ESSAYS ON URBAN AMERICA

THE WALTER PRESCOTT WEBB MEMORIAL LECTURES: IX
Sponsored by The University of Texas at Arlington

THE WALTER PRESCOTT WEBB MEMORIAL LECTURES

ESSAYS ON
URBAN AMERICA

BY

ROBERT F. OAKS

BRUCE I. AMBACHER

RICHARD G. MILLER

RICHARD C. WADE

Introduction by Constance McLaughlin Green

Edited by
Margaret Francine Morris and Elliott West

UNIVERSITY OF TEXAS PRESS • AUSTIN & LONDON

Grateful acknowledgment is made to the Right Honourable
the Earl of Dartmouth for permission to quote from the
Dartmouth Papers in the Staffordshire County Record
Office, Stafford, England.

Library of Congress Cataloging in Publication Data
Main entry under title:

Essays on urban America.

   (The Walter Prescott Webb memorial lectures; 9)
   Includes bibliographies.
   1. Municipal government—United States—History—
Addresses, essays, lectures. 2. Cities and towns—
United States—History—Addresses, essays, lectures.
I. Oaks, Robert F., 1942–   II. Morris, Margaret
Francine, 1938–   ed. III. West, Elliott, 1945–
ed. IV. Series.
JS309.E77   320.9'73   74-31058
ISBN 0-292-72011-4

CONTENTS

PREFACE

The ninth annual Walter Prescott Webb Memorial Lectures were held on March 28, 1974, at the University of Texas at Arlington. The theme, "On Urban America," startled those casual Webb students who think of him as a "western" historian in the sense that he wrote of the frontier American west. His last major work, *The Great Frontier*, challenged us to look beyond the end of the western frontier. In his concluding chapter, Webb counseled us not to feel that we are now "bereft of a challenge and an opportunity." Rather, he said, "we have a different challenge and perhaps an even greater opportunity for achievement. . . . We should not be so obtuse as to believe that the means of management are the same as those of conquest, or that frontier institutions will necessarily serve a metropolitan society. Our challenge consists in finding out what modifications should be made, and our opportunity will come in making them. Our inspiration may come from history, in looking back to the early sixteenth century when the lamp was lifted beside the golden door of the Great Frontier to change the destiny of mankind."*

These essays deal with challenge. Robert F. Oaks examines a

* Walter Prescott Webb, *The Great Frontier* (Austin: University of Texas Press, 1964), p. 418.

city occupied by foreign troops, Philadelphia in the midst of the American Revolution. How did the citizens react? Did civic institutions continue to function? What of the daily needs of food, fuel, and commerce? Drawing on diaries and letters, as well as secondary materials, he gives us an overview of one of the most cosmopolitan cities in the American colonies coping with the immediate physical results of the drive toward independence.

Nearly fifty years later, Andrew Jackson's attacks upon the Second National Bank posed a perplexing dilemma to Philadelphia Democrats. Should they follow their president, the recent recipient of so sweeping a popular mandate, or should they support Nicholas Biddle and the Bank, so crucial to the city's economy and influence? Bruce I. Ambacher demonstrates the effect of this struggle upon the leadership and rank and file of the Democracy. As younger leaders, faithful to the chief executive, took command, they turned increasingly to modern political tactics, such as mass rallies, slogans, distribution of handbills and pamphlets. From this turmoil grew a party more mature and more familiar to our modern eyes.

At the turn of the twentieth century, Fort Worth was a small city between the farms and the range land, without major industry. Richard G. Miller examines the efforts of local business and professional men to discard the familiar ward system for the "efficient" commission form of city government. These reformers sought to reduce taxes, "streamline" city procedures, and place civic authority in the hands of the better educated and fairly well-to-do business and professional classes. This, they felt, was essential if Fort Worth was to lose its "cow town" image, attract industry, and step briskly into the twentieth century. Such "reforms," however, also posed disturbing questions about the role of popular participation in urban politics.

The well-known urban historian Richard C. Wade chooses to

look at the hazards of carrying historical analogies too far in making public policy. We hear constantly that "history shows us" or "history demonstrates" that "A" will lead to "B." Wade illustrates one of the dangers of this approach, taking as his example the immigrant and black experiences in American cities. City fathers and government planners assumed that the twentieth-century rush of blacks to northern urban centers would duplicate that of nineteenth-century European immigrants—in two generations, up and out of the ghettoes. This has not happened. Wade suggests that the wrong analogy was selected in the formulation of policy, that the post–Civil War experience of a southern city, such as Atlanta, more accurately indicated what would happen in Chicago, Philadelphia, New York, and Boston. His informal essay concludes with a number of suggestions for policy makers today if they truly intend to remove the undissolved lumps from the urban melting pot.

It is our pleasant duty to thank everyone who has contributed to each lecture series—our colleagues, students, university staff, and friends. To the lecturers for their work, to the Press for its patience, on behalf of the Webb Lectures Committee, the Department of History, and the University of Texas at Arlington, our thanks.

It has been customary in the past for an acquaintance of Dr. Webb to write a tribute to him as a preface to each volume of this series. In his introduction of one of the morning speakers, Professor George Wolfskill delivered a brief but eloquent tribute to his former teacher. The editors believe Professor Wolfskill's remarks capture the importance of Dr. Webb as a scholar and as a man:

"The death of Walter Prescott Webb in an automobile accident near Austin eleven years ago, March 8, 1963, ended an association of more than forty years with the University of Texas at Austin. But his passing meant more than the loss of a veteran

teacher. As president of the Organization of American Historians and also as president of the American Historical Association, Walter Webb was accorded the highest recognition that
the history profession could bestow. As a prize-winning author,
he attained international stature. His first important book, entitled *The Great Plains*, was considered in some quarters the
most provocative book in American history written in the first
half of the twentieth century. His last major work, entitled
The Great Frontier, was described by Dr. Ray Billington of the
Huntington Library as having 'presented the historical profession with one of the most challenging ideas of the century and
laid the basis for either a controversy of major magnitude or a
reinterpretation of modern history.'

" 'It may well turn out,' wrote one commentator at the time
of Professor Webb's death, 'that Walter Prescott Webb wrote
the most important book that was written anywhere in the world
this century.'

"All of this praise and more was achieved by a man who had
never received a high school diploma, who had left the cruel
and barren land of West Texas to become a universal man.

"His death also meant the loss of a friend. Each of us who
was associated in any way with Professor Webb has his own
memories, stories, anecdotes to relate and cherished encounters
with Dr. Webb, sometimes in the most obscure places. But
whatever the nature of those memories, all of us meet in common accord that here indeed was a great and good man, and
we shall not soon see his kind again."

Margaret Francine Morris
Elliott West

INTRODUCTION
by Constance McLaughlin Green

Today the topics that fall into the general category of American urban history are enormously varied. A mere glance at the program for the 1974 meeting of the Organization of American Historians bears testimony to that truth, as does a scanning of the issues of the Urban History Group *Newsletter* over the last decade. The reasons for this proliferation of monographs on urban themes are clear enough: Students trained in a half-dozen disciplines have come to realize that "urban history is a big tent" covering many kinds of human experience. The population of practically all American cities has long been heterogeneous, differing in ethnic origin or race, religious faith, mundane aspirations, teachability, occupations, wealth, and place in the pecking order. The result is inevitably a diversity of attitudes and interests in every community. And the larger the number of inhabitants the more complex the interrelationships are likely to be.

While the use of computers to tabulate information that can be assembled in statistical form has greatly reduced the drudgery of many research tasks, particularly for the demographer, a good many historical theses pursuing the quality of city life remain dependent on other types of evidence, notably diaries; personal correspondence; newspaper articles; municipal, state, or federal reports; paintings and photographs of street scenes, people, and structures; collections of artifacts; and word-of-mouth reminiscences. Furthermore, it is well to remember that statements of opinion and what people believed to be true may be as valuable in portraying the nature of city life at a given period as a more factually accurate account. Enumeration of the householders packed into New York tenement houses in 1860 or, say, 1900 may give a less vivid idea of the urban jungle than does Rebecca Harding Davis's short story entitled "Life in the Iron Mills," depicting conditions in Wheeling, Virginia, just before the Civil War. Certainly compilations of figures rarely convey feelings of human misery or human joy.

The first three of the four essays composing this ninth volume of the Walter Prescott Webb Memorial Lectures do not draw upon impersonal, computerized data. The authors rely in the main upon literary rather than statistical sources and present their findings in traditional narrative fashion. Indeed "Cliometrics" seem to be ill-suited to the subject matter of these studies: The first deals with the British occupation of Philadelphia in 1777–1778 and Gen. Sir William Howe's endeavor to win friends and influence leading Americans to reaffirm their allegiance to the Crown; the next two papers explore special phases of municipal politics in nineteenth- and early twentieth-century America. The fourth essay, a comparison of the black with immigrant adjustments to urban America, is a bird of another feather: it wings over a century and more of time and over not just one or two but scores of large American cities, and, though population tallies differentiated by race, tax lists, and residential locations identified by black and white provide considerable statistical substantiation of the author's central thesis, the principal tool he employs in interpreting his evidence is social psychology rather than mathematical enumeration.

Robert Oaks, in discussing Philadelphia under military rule, focuses his attention on the day-by-day effects upon citizens' lives, but he also describes the problems confronting General Howe and his subordinates, problems heightened by Howe's wish to conciliate Americans who could be weaned from support of the rebel cause. The difficulty of quartering 20,000 troops in a city where housing for some 23,000 civilians had been insufficient in peacetime, the inadequacy of sanitation and the spread of disease, the frequent occurrence of brawling and disorderliness in public places, and the inflationary prices of all necessities quickly created tensions that worsened with every month. General Howe early established a superintendency for the civilian government of the city and put Joseph Galloway, a staunch loyalist, in complete charge. But good intentions were not enough. Local administrators became increasingly harried. Neither General Howe, Superintendent Galloway, nor any other high-ranking official, however, had to endure the privations that were the common lot of the "lower orders." It was the city's working classes that suffered most from the shortages of food, fuel, housing, and lack of medical care during the months of military occupation.

In view of Oaks's avowed intention of examining "the impact of war upon the American people," readers of this essay may feel disappointment at finding no comparison of Philadelphians' experiences with those of Bostonians, Newporters, Charlestonians, or New Yorkers. For three out of four of these cities fared far worse at the hands of their captors than did the Pennsylvania metropolis. Only New York derived benefits from serving for seven years as British army headquarters. But illuminating as the discussion of such contrasts might be, its elaboration would require time that the speaker on the lecture platform can seldom afford. Robert Oaks's account of Philadelphia in 1777–1778, as it stands, presents enough interesting details rarely mentioned in histories of the American Revolution to make his paper rewarding.

If the story of the "Bank War" of the Jacksonian era at first appears to be a twice- and thrice-told tale familiar in its every particular to students of American economic history and partisan politics, a look at Bruce Ambacher's analysis of the effects of the word battles fought in the City of Brotherly Love in the early 1830's may nevertheless lead to a refreshing surprise. Chiefly by scrutinizing the personal correspondence of scores of articulate men, Philadelphians and others, Ambacher manages to trace the gradual alignment of public opinion on public monetary policies and on the perpetuation of what Jackson supporters labeled "the monster monopoly." Ambacher's research, moreover, outlines the way in which the prolonged controversy contributed to changes in the political tactics of city voters: their growing reliance, for example, on petitions, mass meetings, and popular slogans as part of the paraphernalia of urban election campaigns. In this second-largest city of the United States with an increasingly diversified ethnic population, the politics of self-government, in which naturalized immigrants and all native-born adult males except Negroes and felons could share, took on new importance.

The third article in this volume moves the scene to a small Texas city at the opening of the twentieth century when leading businessmen launched a determined drive to promote the growth of Fort Worth by introducing "efficiency" into local government. Here, as elsewhere, efficiency meant to its advocates the paring down or elimination of the democratic procedures whereby voters of the working classes expressed their wishes and lent their support to ward bosses. Reformers, eager to reduce taxes and vest power in the hands of the well-educated and relatively well-to-do minority composed of bankers, manufacturers, and members of the professions, considered the substitution of a commission form of city administration a virtual must if Fort Worth was to attract new business and take a major place among the great cities of Texas. Step by step Richard Miller describes how the local electorate and the state legislature were finally induced to discard the familiar arrangement ensuring each ward representation of its own interests on the city council, in short, to sacrifice neighborhood participation in municipal decision making in order to achieve the desideratum of bigness. The exposition is at once amusing and mildly distressing in its portrayal of political naïveté. Far more sophisticated cities than Fort Worth, Pittsburgh, for one, similarly adopted new charters calculated to strengthen the voice in city affairs of supposedly enlightened city promoters, only to discover later that excessively rapid industrial growth and constant emphasis on "progress" could have unhappy consequences. It is today a well-known but thought-provoking conclusion.

Richard C. Wade's lecture, "Historical Analogies and Public Policy: The Black and Immigrant Experience in Urban America," analyzes the degree to which historians' errors of judgment may have misdirected public policy in the making during the World War I era when rural blacks began to move cityward in massive numbers. Historians and social scientists, Professor Wade argues, tended to assume that the black immigrant to the city could and would follow the pattern set by generations of European immigrants, as members of one ethnic group after another gradually made their way upward out of the slums where they had first landed and remained in their early years in the United States. That for decades the racial segregation existing de facto if not de jure in most American cities barred blacks from pursuing the course open to all manner of European newcomers was an idea that even thoughtful whites were slow to acknowledge until the rising volume of black protest obliged them to rethink their positions.

Wade's discussion of the conflicts and dilemmas of the late 1960's and early 1970's is at once forceful and judicious. Inasmuch as black neighborhoods almost invariably abut on low-income white residential areas, and the white families living on the edge of the ghetto are always among the least educated, the poorest, and the most insecure people in the United States, the chances for violent confrontations in the inner city intensify year by year. Meanwhile the suburbanites, the persons best qualified by education and material resources to quench the hatreds and loosen "the white noose about black downtown," have generally remained aloof, albeit critical, of both radical black militance and white blue-collar backlashing. This "most delicate and explosive" problem facing urban America today can only be resolved, Richard Wade believes, by inducing all ranks of society to share in breaking down the walls of the ghetto and dispersing low-income families, white as well as black, among more affluent neighborhoods. His suggestions of how to achieve this difficult result are well worth reading.

ESSAYS ON URBAN AMERICA

The City under Military Occupation: Philadelphia, 1777–1778

BY ROBERT F. OAKS

THE BICENTENNIAL OF THE American Revolution and the resulting increased interest in the nation's birth will lead historians inevitably to delve more deeply into aspects of that movement that have been overlooked or underemphasized. There have been many detailed studies of military and diplomatic topics, but very few works detail the impact of war on the American people. The presence of British armies, even when they were not fighting, profoundly influenced American attitudes and may have been as important as military and diplomatic factors in the outcome of the war. In cities, occupying armies, even when relatively benign, can do more to harm their cause when they are not fighting than they can by losing a battle. Such was the case with British behavior in Philadelphia during the winter of 1777–1778.

The fall of 1777 was a discouraging period for the would-be independent United States of America. With New York City occupied by the British forces of Gen. Sir William Howe, the plan for isolating New England by driving northward from that city, while at the same time pushing south from Canada, seemed certain to succeed. The city of Philadelphia, largest in North America, seat of the Continental Congress, and de facto capital of the emerging nation, braced itself as it became clear that Howe intended to occupy it, too.

Most of his officers advised him to give as much support as possible to the impending invasion from Canada, but Howe decided instead to take most of his army from New York to Philadelphia. Loyalists, such as Joseph Galloway, former speaker of the Pennsylvania Assembly, assured the British commander that his troops would be welcomed warmly by a substantial portion of the population. Howe planned to place the city under a loyalist government and use it as a base to move into Virginia during the winter of 1778, sweeping through the lower south by the following spring. The rebellion would be crushed and the ungrateful colonists returned to their rightful place in the British Empire.[1]

Howe's scheme never materialized. Gen. John Burgoyne surrendered to American Gen. Horatio Gates at Saratoga in October, destroying the plan to detach New England, and Howe, though he took Philadelphia with ease in September, discovered that the problems involved in occupying this city were greater than he had been led to believe.

If name calling could stop armies, General Howe never would have gotten close to Philadelphia. As the British intentions became clear, newspapers tried to rally Americans to the defense of the city. If the British were defeated while attempting to take Philadelphia, the newspapers claimed, independence would be assured. If the British succeeded, however, Americans faced a horrible fate. The British, one paper predicted, would bring "rapine, devastation and burnings."[2] Thomas Paine, in his "American Crisis," called upon Pennsylvanians to follow the example of other states—he was a bit vague as to just which ones he had in mind—and drive off the invaders.[3]

The brave rhetoric, however, neither stopped the advance of Howe's army from the Chesapeake Bay toward Philadelphia nor rallied many Americans. On the contrary, feverish preparations were made for evacuation. Pennsylvania authorities hastily arrested leading Quakers, whose pacifist religious beliefs left them open to the charge that they were supporting the enemy, and sent them to Virginia.[4]

By September 19, Howe's army was so close that the Continental Congress decided to abandon the city. One delegate left in such haste that he did not bother to saddle his horse. Rumors that the Americans would burn the city rather than let it fall to the British increased the tension of residents.[5] By the twenty-third, American military authorities ordered all boats in the Delaware River prepared for immediate sailing and all provisions and supplies removed to prevent them from falling into British hands.[6] On the twenty-fifth, Howe, only five miles from the city, asked Pennsylvania authorities to inform residents that, if they remained in their homes, they would not be harmed. Patrols were set up that night to watch for fire after two men were arrested for saying they intended to burn the city.[7]

The much rumored fires never materialized. Supporters of the Revolution left the city, taking with them, according to one Tory, everything of value. Then at 8 A.M. on the twenty-sixth, the first British troops, led by Lord Charles Cornwallis, entered the city to the accompaniment of band music. Since all the extreme Whigs had gone, the occupation took place without incident. Benjamin Towne's *Pennsylvania Evening Post*, which had so recently exhorted Americans to rise up against British tyranny, suddenly discovered that the British were really saviors. Robert Proud, the future Tory historian, remarked that the British forces brought a degree of order and tranquility unknown in Philadelphia for years. Joseph Galloway, who accompanied the troops into the city, later reported, probably with exaggeration, that there were "acclamations of joy in every street."[8]

Once in possession of the city, the British faced problems that would continue to plague them throughout their nine months of occupation and ultimately cast doubt on the wisdom of Howe's decision. The mere presence of an army of twenty thousand— nearly equal in size to the civilian population of Philadelphia— created enormous problems of housing and supply for civilian and soldier alike. In addition, Howe had to keep his largely idle soldiers from harming lives and property, "the dreadful consequences," one Philadelphia Tory admitted, "of an army however friendly." Finally, Howe wanted to restore civilian rule and business conditions to as near normal as possible.[9]

Controlling the troops to prevent them from alienating residents continuously troubled the British from the very beginning. Within two days, Robert Morton, the Tory diarist, complained of British troops looting his country estate. A British officer assured Morton that the troops would be punished severely if caught, and that one soldier had already received four hundred lashes for a similar crime. But a few days later, soldiers took two loads of hay from Morton's pasture. Still later, he discovered one hundred Hessians plundering the countryside of cabbages and potatoes. Morton saved his own crop only by requesting and receiving protection of an army guard. In spite of Howe's statements that loyal inhabitants would be protected, Morton noticed in despair that these incidents continued. He eventually lost fifty bushels of potatoes, and most of his neighbors lost even more.[10]

As Morton recognized, the army's plundering not only threatened the loss of crops but also, and more importantly, undermined support for the British. What particularly bothered

Morton was the unnecessary effect of this "irksome" conduct. If only the troops would pay for confiscated products, they could have both food and the "good wishes of the people." But, he lamented, "contrary conduct . . . produced contrary effects," and endangered the success of the entire British campaign.[11]

In addition to their activities in the countryside, the soldiers also plagued city dwellers. Elizabeth Drinker, whose Quaker husband had been exiled to Virginia, reported that a soldier came into her house and demanded blankets. When she refused, the soldier simply went upstairs and took one, saying he was merely borrowing it on General Howe's orders.[12] Complaints about these incidents prompted Howe to resort to harsh measures, especially when it became clear that many soldiers were stealing, not only to supply their own needs but also to sell the stolen goods. He threatened "the most exemplary Punishment" for anyone found guilty of theft or of buying stolen goods from soldiers.[13]

The threat was futile. Plundering continued and Howe received daily complaints. Realizing the seriousness of the problem, Howe in desperation asked all officers to cooperate in ending this "shameful, and unsoldierlike behavior." Night patrols were ordered to apprehend "soldiers or disorderly persons." But even these measures proved useless.[14]

In addition to stealing, General Howe and the good citizens of Philadelphia had to contend with another age-old problem. The British and Hessian troops, lonely and far away from home, inevitably sought companionship with the young ladies of the city. And sometimes the young ladies themselves did the seeking. Elizabeth Drinker could not keep her servant girl away from the gate of their home after the soldiers arrived. When the girl finally ran off with one of the soldiers, Mrs. Drinker was almost relieved.[15]

These activities also caused more serious problems. By the

end of the year, newspapers were advertising such medicines as Dr. Yeldall's "Antiveneral Essence," which was supposed to cure "the disease in all its degrees, and in such a manner that the patient need not be hindered from his business, or his condition be made known to his most intimate acquaintance." Printed instructions were included "so that no questions need be asked." A real bargain at two dollars![16] There were also advertisements for "Hannay's Preventive" for "a certain disorder" and "Keyser's famous Pills, so well known all over Europe, and in this and the neighbouring provinces, for their superior efficacy and peculiar mildness, in perfectly eradicating every degree of a certain disease." The same shop, by the way, also sold "Dr. Ryan's incomparable worm-destroying sugar plumbs," but presumably that disorder could not be blamed on the British army.[17]

Since there were many more soldiers than available young women, two enterprising soldiers went so far as to advertise for "*a young woman*, to act in the capacity of housekeeper and who can occasionally put her hand *to anything. Extravagent wages* will be given, and *no character* required."[18] This type of activity was impossible to control, and General Howe, who himself kept a mistress in Philadelphia, did very little except plead for better behavior and try to regulate the sale of liquor to cool amorous passions.[19]

Soldiers continued to enjoy themselves at the expense of Philadelphia's citizens. Even a group of Howe's officers mistreated several unarmed watchmen one evening as they were attempting to patrol the city. Howe fumed about such "illiberal outrages" and on more than one occasion used the whip in an attempt to control his soldiers, but there is little evidence that he had any success in calming twenty thousand bored men.[20]

The army's attempt to find food and shelter proved an equally insoluble problem. Perhaps more than anything else, this search

alienated citizen from soldier. Foraging for food in the countryside was annoying, but commodity shortages and inflation in the
city inconvenienced Philadelphians far more. The Whigs took
all the supplies they could carry when they left the city, and the
first few weeks of occupation were especially grim. Within three
weeks of the British arrival, one staunch Tory confided to his
diary that citizens faced the "prospect of starvation." Supplies
were "very scarce" and those that existed were very expensive.[21]
Robert Proud and other Tories blamed the shortages on the
Whigs who took everything of value with them and then devas-
tated the surrounding countryside.[22] For a while the American
army prevented the British from supplying the city. Few residents had supplies in their homes to last more than a month,
and a temporary blockade of the Delaware River made the situation even more precarious.[23] By December, James Allen estimated that shortages had increased the price of most necessities
tenfold in the two and one-half months of occupation.[24] Even
Gen. George Washington, camped nearby at Valley Forge, worried about shortages in Philadelphia. The worst sufferers, he
learned, were prisoners held by the British. Some of them had
enlisted in the British army to avoid starvation.[25]

Throughout the war the British made heroic efforts to supply
their troops across three thousand miles of ocean, but the diffi-
culties of this task were enormous. Daniel Weir, the British
commissary at Philadelphia during the occupation, was feeding
36,000 people and 3,147 horses each day by January 1778. Since
there were no storehouses, all provisions were piled in open
fields "guarded by sentries of sometimes questionable loyalty."
The troops brought six hundred tons of oats and hay from the
area around Philadelphia; with an equal amount expected from
Rhode Island, Weir hoped to get the army through the winter.[26]
The horses alone required twenty-four tons of hay per day.[27]
Weir thought he could meet that demand, but he was worried

by the shortage of rum. With every soldier entitled to one-sixth of a quart per day and an extra four ounces in "inclement weather," Weir was hard pressed to supply this essential product. The army brought 100,000 gallons from New York, and Weir had ordered an additional 100,000 gallons, but a shortage of lumber made it difficult to build casks to keep it in.[28]

Like food, wood was an essential product in short supply. As November temperatures turned chilly, Elizabeth Drinker complained about the high price of firewood and the near impossibility of getting it cut and hauled.[29] The shortage also plagued the army. Each regiment had to gather its own firewood, and one hundred troops were dispatched each day to protect the woodcutters. With every fireplace in the city burning an estimated three-eighths of a cord per week, wood remained scarce even after food became relatively plentiful.[30]

Shortages and inflation inevitably brought black marketing.[31] As usual, the poor suffered most under these conditions. The Fourth Street Quaker Meeting House and Carpenter's Hall were used to house the poor, but the facilities became completely inadequate as the situation grew worse.[32] By December, the problem of shortages was so acute that leading Quakers, who were certainly not the poorest segment of Philadelphia society, wrote their co-religionists in Ireland begging for support. They asked for immediate shipment of beef, pork, butter, wheat, cheese, grain, bacon, coal, and other articles, promising to pay when they could. As a result of this request, subscriptions for the relief of Philadelphia began in both England and Ireland.[33]

The situation improved gradually and prices started to fall. A shipment from England dropped the price of beef by nearly one-third in December, and, by January, the overall drop in prices was termed "very remarkable."[34] There is little evidence of anyone actually starving during the occupation, but, even after the Delaware River was reopened to shipping, the problems of supply and shortages of food remained. As late as March 1778, Robert Proud, a Tory but also a businessman, planned to profit from shortages and high prices by having his brother send a quick shipment of goods from England.[35]

A lack of currency during the occupation exacerbated the problem of shortages. British entry into the city automatically invalidated any Continental currency on hand. The old Pennsylvania colonial currency was legal tender once again, but many merchants and shopkeepers were reluctant to take any kind of paper money and insisted on specie. Several citizens began a drive to support paper currency, and many women vowed not to purchase goods with specie.[36] But this campaign stalled when British merchants, who arrived with the fleet when the river was reopened, absolutely refused to accept any kind of paper money. The campaign was also stymied by certain residents who bought products they needed with gold, "thus purchasing," Robert Morton complained, "momentary gratifications at the expense of the Public." People who had no gold or silver, Morton predicted, would soon be "reduced to beggary and want."[37]

Newspapers also excoriated those who refused to accept paper currency. They were accused of trying to "starve the widow and orphan, and sacrifice a whole country to rise upon their ruin."[38] So great was the shortage of hard money that even the British troops were paid half in specie and half in Pennsylvania currency.[39] When pressure to get merchants to accept paper money failed, some citizens even suggested that residents follow the example of the rebel Continental Congress and agree to boycott all goods until the policy changed. Lest they be accused of "reviving . . . unlawful associations," however, this proposal was deemed "a virtuous resolution to adhere to the old established laws of the land."[40] The boycott never materialized, but the controversy over the use of paper money and the ensuing hardships continued, and many a Philadelphian may have

wondered if the British were really the saviors they had anticipated.

In addition to shortages of food, wood, and money, housing
for the army was also difficult to find. Vacant homes and public
buildings were filled first, but inevitably private homes were
used and just as inevitably some people resented the intrusion
of soldiers. Even without the resentment, the crowded conditions created health and sanitation problems and increased bur-
glary and petty larceny. When storage buildings were emptied
and turned into barracks, many Philadelphians unwisely stored
such combustible items as pitch, tar, turpentine, hay, straw,
and fodder in their attics and elsewhere in their homes. Insur-
ance agents felt it necessary to remind their clients that policies
usually did not cover fires resulting from stored flammable
goods.[41]

Elizabeth Drinker's experience was probably typical of many
Philadelphians. Several days after the British entered the city,
an officer asked Mrs. Drinker to take a wounded soldier into her
home. She refused, pleading the absence of her husband. In
December, however, Maj. John Cramond called and asked permission to move in. Again Mrs. Drinker tried to beg off, but
the major convinced her that an officer would provide protection. And, since "he behaved with much politeness," she re-
lented. At the end of the month the major, one servant, two
horses, and a cow moved in. Cramond's two other servants
boarded with a neighbor.[42]

Before long, Mrs. Drinker reported with some relief, the
"thoughtful, sober young" major had become one of the family.
Eventually he had three horses, three cows, two sheep, two tur-
keys, and several fowl in the Drinker stable. The major kept to
himself in the two front parlors of the house. Occasionally other
officers dined with him, but their behavior was good and they
always left at a decent hour. On other occasions the major drank

tea with the Drinker family. Mrs. Drinker reported to her exiled husband that there was neither "Swareing or Gameing" under their roof.[43] Henry Drinker, however, helplessly separated from his family, was enraged when he learned that the British had forced the young officer into his home.[44]

Major Cramond's quarters were undoubtedly much better than those of the average soldier. In all, there were twenty-six battalions in Philadelphia. The State House (Independence Hall) was one of the better barracks available, and five companies lived there "in a most comfortable Manner." Other troops stayed in the public school house and in every other available building. Two Presbyterian churches were converted into hospitals for the sick, and St. Paul's churchyard became a burial ground for those who died. The dead were thrown into large pits, without coffins, and, after several rains, arms and legs projected above the ground.[45]

General Howe's quarters were quite satisfactory. He lived in a house in High Street, which was later the residence of President Washington, and rode through the town in the carriage of Israel Pemberton, another of the Quakers exiled in Virginia. Other high-ranking officers enjoyed only slightly less comfortable accommodations.[46]

Howe was relatively successful in his attempt to place city government in civilian hands. The government of pre-Revolutionary Philadelphia had been practically feudal in structure. A closed self-perpetuating corporation handled most of the city's problems in a more or less satisfactory arrangement that excluded ordinary citizens from city government.[47] Consequently, it was not very difficult to set up civilian rule that would satisfy most residents, since they had never participated in the government anyway.

For the first two months of occupation, martial law was instituted with little distinction made between running the city and commanding the army. Samuel Shoemaker, the former city treasurer, acted as mayor during this period, but with little authority. In these first few weeks, the government concentrated on persuading residents to take an oath of allegiance to the king, raising troops from Tory sympathizers, and preserving the peace. Howe increased the civilian night watch from 17 to 120 men who served in rotation and exacted forced loans of up to ten pounds from each citizen to pay for the service.[48]

After this initial two-month period, Philadelphia was ruled through a series of proclamations issued by either Howe or by Joseph Galloway, who was appointed to administer the city. The choice of Galloway was one that Howe later had good reason to regret, for the two men engaged in a bitter controversy in England over Howe's strategy, ability, and goals. But that was in the future, and at the time the selection of Galloway seemed both logical and auspicious. As the former speaker of the Pennsylvania Assembly, a close associate of Benjamin Franklin, and a power in Pennsylvania politics for many years, Galloway was the most prominent of Pennsylvania Tories who had political experience. Howe must have been quite pleased at Galloway's support for the king.[49]

A few days after the British entered Philadelphia, Howe placed Galloway in charge of administering the oath of allegiance to the king. Within a month, however, Galloway had so many other chores that he appointed Enoch Story as his assistant in charge of administering the oath.[50] Howe then put Galloway in complete control of the civilian government and appointed him to the newly created offices of superintendent general of the police and superintendent of imports and exports.[51]

Howe's letter of instructions to Galloway made it clear that the general was much more concerned with the port of Philadelphia than he was with the city. Galloway was instructed to make sure that goods entering the port did not fall into the hands of the rebels or their supporters.[52] Galloway's civilian duties included the preservation of the "security of the inhabitants, the suppression of vice and licentiousness, the preservation of the peace, the support of the poor, the maintenance of the nightly watch and lamps, and the regulation of the markets and ferries, with other matters in which the oeconomy [*sic*], peace, and good order of the city of Philadelphia and its environs are concerned."[53] Such was the extent of municipal government in the eighteenth century.

Galloway's appointment produced mixed reactions. Ambrose Serle, secretary to General Howe's brother, Adm. Lord Richard Howe, believed that "no Man [could] be more fit for the Purpose at this critical Time."[54] Anne Penn, wife of former Governor John Penn, however, bitterly remembered Galloway's long campaign before the Revolution to remove Pennsylvania from the control of the proprietary Penn family and place it directly under the Crown. She was bothered by his "very uncommon powers" and feared that he would use them against the proprietary interest. She supposed that Howe was unacquainted "with the real character on Politics of Mr. Galloway when he appointed him to his present office."[55]

Mrs. Penn may have been correct in her assessment of Galloway's potential harm. He long had advocated closer ties between the colonies and the Crown and possibly saw his position of superintendent general as an opportunity to bring about his dreams of a more satisfactory Anglo-American relationship once the rebellion ended.[56]

Howe's motives for appointing Galloway, however, were both political and military. Though he later claimed that he had been misled as to the extent of Galloway's popularity and influence in Pennsylvania, Howe believed that Galloway would bring support for the occupying forces, would be a source of intelligence information, and would be able to raise a considerable number of American troops to fight for the British cause. Most of the general's hopes proved unfounded. Before long, Howe concluded that his superintendent's ideas were "visionary," his intelligence "ill-founded or . . . exaggerated," and "that very few of the men he did raise were Americans."[57] Yet, even with these negative qualities, Howe later admitted that Galloway was "not deficient" in his conduct as superintendent general, and so he allowed him to maintain this lucrative position with an annual salary of almost £800 sterling.[58]

Galloway began his new job with a flurry of activity. Shortly after assuming his office, he issued a proclamation regulating the sale of liquor, molasses, salt, and medicine. A few weeks later he ordered that the 8:30 P.M. curfew should be more strictly enforced. Anyone out after that time would be subject to questioning and imprisonment. Also, anyone out at night had to carry a lantern.[59]

Galloway was also concerned with the physical appearance of the city. By January of the new year, he noted that the unswept "foot pavements" of the city were so dirty as to cause "great annoyance and inconvenience." Galloway, therefore, ordered residents to rake and sweep the dirt into the streets every Saturday or face a five-shilling fine.[60] Apparently this order worked all too well. A few weeks later Galloway noted that the streets were "much incommoded with Mud, dirt, and other filth to the great annoyance and inconvenience of the inhabitants." Consequently, all residents were ordered to rake all debris into piles in front of their homes or shops during the last week of each month, presumably to be hauled away. The penalty for noncompliance was hiked to twenty shillings.[61]

Another type of filth potentially caused even greater hazards. Citizens were not sweeping their chimneys often enough, creating the threat of fire. Galloway declared that fires in chimneys that had not been swept during the previous month would result in fines of twenty shillings. If the chimney had been swept during the preceding month, then the fine would be levied against the sweeper for doing an insufficient job.[62]

As superintendent general, Galloway also puzzled over the prevention of black marketing. Some citizens purchased goods at the docks of the city before they could be carried to the market place. When a shortage followed, these goods would be sold at "an extortionate price." Galloway ordered that no one purchase food with the intention of reselling it. The penalty for violating this regulation was confiscation of the goods involved, part of them going to the poor of the city, and the rest to the informer or person who had seized the provisions. In case of dispute before a magistrate, the burden of proof would be on the accused.[63]

Galloway made other provisions for the poor. By February 1778, with all funds for the relief of the indigent exhausted and with no tax assessors "as formerly" to replenish these funds, he called for donations from residents and appointed several persons in each ward to collect the money.[64]

Gradually, conditions in the occupied city returned to near normal. Those Philadelphians who were separated from members of their families found life difficult, but for most residents conditions grew more and more usual. The College of Philadelphia reopened for classes in November and requested all "students and scholars" (the distinction between the two terms is unclear) to attend nine o'clock classes in philosophy and Latin.[65] The two public libraries remained open, though one British official considered this a mixed blessing, since they were "furnished chiefly with modern books, and are disgraced with many Productions of our lowest Authors, even down to Novels and Romances."[66] Shops reopened as supplies began to filter into the city after the river was cleared. Shopkeepers who remained ran their own establishments, and British merchants and artisans who came with the army ran the businesses of those Philadelphians who had fled the city.[67]

Besides intellectual and business activities, there were many other diversions during the winter to occupy soldier and citizen alike. British officers organized a theater as they had done the previous year in New York. Using the facilities of the existing Southwark Theatre, the officers, with military discipline, created the best productions of the colonial period. The first play, a somewhat off-color comedy, was entitled *The Wonder: A Woman Keeps a Secret*. The opening was delayed when no copies of the script could be found in Quaker Philadelphia, but, after its first performance in January, it was repeated nearly every Monday night until the following May. The amateur company produced more than a dozen other plays, including some Shakespeare. General Howe attended most of the performances and sat in the "Royal Box" with his mistress. Maj. John Andre played leading roles in several productions, though his true fame would come later from a different kind of acting.[68]

Dancing was also popular that winter. The Whig diarist Christopher Marshall wrote with disgust of "our enemies revelling in balls, attended with every degree of luxury and excess in the city." Marshall hoped that news of such revelry would not spread abroad lest Europeans take it as evidence that the British had won and Americans were afraid to fight any longer.[69] Meanwhile, Washington's army lived in far less luxurious quarters a few miles away.

Even Quakers, with many of their leaders still in exile, managed to live relatively normal lives. Unlike the situation that had prevailed when the Whigs held Philadelphia, Quakers received little interference or injury while the British were there. Quakers who lived outside the British protection, however, continued to suffer property confiscation and imprisonment at the hands of Whigs, and as a result many of them fled to the city for protection.[70]

In spite of generally favorable conditions, however, citizens and soldiers alike gradually came to dislike the atmosphere of the occupied city. This was especially true of Hessian troops, but British soldiers as well tired of their surroundings. Most soldiers apparently were impressed with Philadelphia at first. There were many comments about the beautiful public squares, the charming location, and the fertile countryside. The right-angled streets of William Penn's plan gave the city "a very neat appearance in general," though at least one officer believed that the location, between two rivers, was unhealthy.[71]

Other impressions were less than favorable. A Hessian officer, writing to relatives in Germany, claimed that he would not take all of Pennsylvania in exchange for his military commission if it meant he would have to spend the rest of his life there. "And that," he commented sarcastically, "is the promised land, the land flowing with milk and honey, that so many have praised before us." He could not find one resident with a healthy color, because, he surmised, of bad air and water. The people were lacking in mental as well as physical health: ". . . almost all have a quiet madness, an aberration of the mind, which comes from compressed, not heated blood." He suggested that this resulted from the diet, since the food did not have the same strength as German food, the milk was not as rich, and the bread not as good. And, if all this were not bad enough, the countryside was full of wild animals. Bears and wolves, he believed, roamed at will, and there were snakes living along the Schuylkill River. The worst was a "great rattlesnake," which he described as being twelve to sixteen feet long with the ability to kill with a glance. The soldier related the story of a relative of the farmer in whose house he was staying: "He went hunting, saw a bear standing still, aimed, and shot it down; hardly had he come near the bear when he too had to stand still; he stood for a while, fell over, and died. And this due to a rattlesnake which sat on a tall tree." No wonder the poor German wanted nothing to do with this strange place called Pennsylvania.[72]

Six months later, however, this same German officer did find some praiseworthy aspects of Philadelphia. Like many others, he liked the streets intersecting at right angles and the "pleasant appearance" of the houses. He also praised the sidewalks, which he reluctantly admitted were even better than those in his home town. Apparently Galloway's campaign to clean them up succeeded. The officer's opinion of the American people, though, was still fairly low. American conceit was unbearable, "especially . . . the Philadelphian, who thinks there is not more beautiful, wealthy, and prosperous land on earth than their state which is hardly in the bud." Furthermore, American wages were too high, but he supposed this was necessary to get men to work when they could so easily support themselves by farming as little as three hours a day: "For if he works three hours a day in the field, he has twenty-one left to sleep, yawn, breakfast, take a walk, gossip, and gape at the moon: this happy existence he cannot have in the workshop. Figure out for yourself the future epoch of American civilization. For as long as there is still land enough the farmers will not become artists."[73] In a perverse way, this eighteenth-century German officer reveals himself to be a Turnerian.

Not surprisingly, the American opinion of German officers was often not very high either. Indeed, the German commander, General Knyphausen, reportedly spread butter on bread with his thumb, though in other matters he was supposed to be "gentle, and esteemed."[74] Yet, inevitably, occupying armies begin to wear out their welcome even among their friendliest supporters. One observer referred to "the devastation . . . committed in the environs of the city indiscriminately on Whig and Tory property" by the troops. Residents later estimated their losses at more than £187,000 in property damaged during the occupation, plus an estimated £10,000 in debts left behind by British officers.[75]

The decision to leave Philadelphia was a difficult one that was bound to create even more animosity toward the British from former supporters. The decision was not Howe's, but rather the British government's. Stunned by the defeat at Saratoga and by French entry into the conflict, the ministry decided to retrench in the middle colonies in order to concentrate on fighting the French and on holding Canada while waiting for the results of an ill-fated peace overture to the Americans.[76] General Howe was no longer in command of the forces when the order came to evacuate Philadelphia. He had long disagreed with Lord George Germain, the British colonial secretary, and other top ministry officials both as to military strategy and the overall philosophy behind the fighting. Howe had always advocated leniency toward Americans to bring about reconciliation, and from the beginning of the occupation the general had conferred with leading Philadelphians, such as Thomas Willing, in an attempt to achieve that result.[77]

Even while negotiating with Willing, however, the general asked to be relieved from his command because of the lack of support from his superiors.[78] British politics and administrative red tape delayed naming a successor, and Howe was in effect a lame-duck during nearly all the occupation of Philadelphia. In the spring of 1778, however, Gen. Henry Clinton succeeded Howe with instructions to proceed with evacuating the city.

Before Howe sailed for England, however, Philadelphia was the scene of an elaborate farewell party given for the general by his officers. This was the "Mischianza," perhaps the most extravagant party in the entire colonial and Revolutionary period.[79] Seven hundred and fifty invitations were issued for the affair held in Joseph Wharton's mansion on May 18.

The party began in early afternoon with a parade of coaches and carriages through the city to the Delaware River. The guests then boarded boats and sailed down the river toward the mansion. Warships in the harbor, decorated for the occasion, fired salutes as the procession passed. Three flatboats carried bands, which entertained the group as they were rowed down the river to the mansion. A triumphal arch, erected in the center of the lawn, was surrounded by an honor guard displaying British and Hessian colors. Behind the house, a large pavilion decorated with mirrors and chandeliers had been constructed for the affair.

A mock medieval tournament began the entertainment. Young ladies, dressed in Turkish habits, wore in their turbans the articles they intended to bestow on their gallant knights. A trumpet sounded, and several "knights of the blended rose," dressed in white and red silk, entered on grey chargers and saluted the ladies. Another flourish of trumpets, and the challengers, "the knights of the burning mountain," dressed in black and orange, repeated the ceremony. The participants fought with spears, pistols, and swords, to the delight of the audience. Then the dancing began. The Howe brothers, accompanied by fifty-two ladies and gentlemen, proceeded through the triumphal arch into a circle completely surrounded by flags. One Hessian officer declared it "a spectacle one will never forget." The dancing continued, interrupted only by a display of fireworks, until dinner was served at midnight.

The tables held more than a thousand plates and dishes. Twenty-four black slaves in oriental dress with silver collars and bracelets attended to the wishes of the guests. There was more music and innumerable toasts to the king, the Howe brothers, the noble knights, and many others. Then, when the meal was over, dancing resumed until at least four in the morning. General Howe must have considered it a worthy farewell party.[80]

To some Philadelphians, however, the "Mischianza" was disgraceful. Elizabeth Drinker predicted that the day would be remembered for "scenes of folly and vanity." The contrast of this extravagant spectacle with the conditions of the American army at Valley Forge, the exiled Quakers in Virginia, or even the condition of the majority of citizens in the occupied city must have occurred to many people. Even some British officers were "ashamed" by the affair.[81]

A few days after the farewell party, Howe turned over his command to Clinton and sailed to England to face an investigation into his conduct by a Parliamentary committee. By that time, however, preparations to evacuate Philadelphia were already well underway. English merchants who came with the army packed up their goods to leave with the army. Many Philadelphians who had supported the English also prepared to evacuate and one observer compared the atmosphere of the city to "a fair during the last week of business."[82]

The decision to leave was not popular with many people. Some men worried about the psychological effect of giving up this major target at a time when the French had just entered the war and the British were making serious overtures to bring about peace. Leaving Philadelphia without harming the city, it was argued, would look like a retreat. But if the city were destroyed, it would ruin whatever chance of peace that might exist and would place the British in the position of resorting to "the worst Extremes of War."[83]

Joseph Galloway, who was furious at the decision, worried about the effect on Tory sentiment, already declining because of the troops' behavior. In a similar vein, a British general later testified that the evacuation alienated many people, who then took oaths of allegiance to the United States. Another observer commented that Tories "abandoned themselves to a lethargy very nearly bordering on despair."[84]

Galloway suggested that it would be better to storm Washington at Valley Forge to end the rebellion and demoralize Congress rather than lift their spirits by abandoning the city.[85] But the decision was firm. Three months' provisions for five thousand men were loaded on the ships, and by the middle of June the army began the evacuation.[86] Enoch Story left with his family; Joseph Galloway left his wife behind, never to see her again, and headed for life-long exile in England.[87]

On June 18, there were still nine thousand British troops in the city; the next morning "not one red-coat to be seen."[88] On the twentieth, Maj. Gen. Benedict Arnold of the Continental Army declared the city "open . . . and under the usual regulations as in times of peace."[89] The Congress returned July 2, and, on the Fourth, Philadelphia was the scene of a "great fuss" celebrating the anniversary of the Declaration of Independence. Guns and sky rockets provided noise and color to the celebration, though the price of candles was still too high to light up the city in a manner befitting such an event.[90]

Many changes had taken place between the time the British entered Philadelphia in triumph and the time, nine months later, when they left, if not in defeat, at least under a cloud. General Howe had taken the city in anticipation of a quick end to the rebellion. But Philadelphia was not the crucial strategic site he hoped it would be. Neither the Continental Congress nor Washington's army collapsed when they lost Philadelphia. And events in Saratoga, London, and New York worked against Howe's conciliatory program. Furthermore, the attempts to govern an occupied city compounded Howe's problems and in the end turned many of his American supporters against him. The episode provides an example of what one historian recently termed "a political education conducted by military means." Without trying to institute harsh measures, the army managed to take "manipulable, potentially loyal subjects of the crown" and turn many of them into "wary citizens of the United States."[91] Rather than hastening British victory, the occupation of Philadelphia alienated many people from the Tory cause, infuriated those like Galloway who remained loyal, and in the end may have helped prolong the war until the Americans could win.

NOTES

I wish to acknowledge generous research support for this paper from the American Philosophical Society and the Organized Research Fund of the University of Texas at Arlington.

1. Ira D. Gruber, *The Howe Brothers and the American Revolution*, pp. 230–234; Troyer Steele Anderson, *The Command of the Howe Brothers during the American Revolution*, p. 294; John Richard Alden, *The American Revolution, 1775–1783*, pp. 112–114.

2. *Pennsylvania Evening Post*, September 9, 1777; proclamation of Thomas Wharton, Jr., President of Pennsylvania, in ibid., September 11, 1777.

3. Thomas Paine, "The American Crisis," no. 4, in ibid., September 13, 1777.

4. Robert F. Oaks, "Philadelphians in Exile: The Problem of Loyalty during the American Revolution," *Pennsylvania Magazine of History and Biography* (hereinafter *PMHB*) 96 (1972): 298–325. Although Quakers made up only about one-seventh of Philadelphia's population, their economic and political influence far surpassed their numerical significance, making it impossible for Revolutionary leaders to ignore them when they refused to support the war. Though they tried to remain neutral, Quakers were regarded as Tories, and, as Howe's army approached Philadelphia, Pennsylvania's Revolutionary government used obviously false evidence of Quaker support for the British to justify sending twenty of them into exile.

5. "The Diary of Robert Morton," *PMHB* 1 (1877): September 19, 23, 1777, pp. 3–4, 7.

6. Proclamation of Lewis Nicola, *Pennsylvania Evening Post*, September 23, 1777.

7. "The Diary of Robert Morton," *PMHB* 1 (1877): September 25, 1777, p. 7.

8. *Pennsylvania Evening Post*, October 11, 1777; memorandum of Robert Proud, September 29, 1777, Robert Proud's Memoranda, Historical Society of Pennsylvania (hereinafter HSP); Robert Francis Seybolt, "A Contemporary British Account of General Sir William Howe's Military Operations in 1777," *American Antiquarian Society Proceedings*, n.s., 40 (1930): 83; [Joseph Galloway], *Letters to a Nobleman on the Conduct of the War in the Middle Colonies*, p. 22.

9. See "Abstract of Forces under Sir William Howe," October 13, 1777, Colonial Office Papers, class 5, vol. 253, Public Record Office, London (hereinafter C. O. 5/253). The best estimate of Philadelphia's population is in Sam Bass Warner, Jr., *The Private City: Philadelphia*

in Three Periods of Its Growth, p. 225. Warner calculates the population on the eve of the Revolution as 23,739. Since many people fled the city as the British approached, an estimate of approximately 20,000 during the occupation is not unreasonable. Joseph Galloway estimated the population of the city and suburbs in October 1777, as 21,767. See Galloway to Lord Dartmouth, January 23, 1778, in Benjamin Franklin Stevens (ed.), *Facsimiles of Manuscripts in European Archives Relating to America, 1773–1783,* XXIV, 2085. A much larger estimate of 60,000 people, including army, navy, and civilian residents, was made by a British staff officer in May 1778. See G. D. Scull (ed.), "Journal of Captain John Montresor, July 1, 1777, to July 1, 1778, Chief Engineer of the British Army," *PMHB* 6 (1882): 287.

10. "The Diary of Robert Morton," *PMHB* 1 (1877): September 28, October 19, 1777, pp. 9, 19–20.

11. Ibid., October 24, 1777, pp. 23–24.

12. "Extracts from the Journal of Mrs. Henry Drinker, of Philadelphia, from September 25, 1777, to July 4, 1778," *PMHB* 13 (1889): November 5, 1777, p. 301 (hereinafter Elizabeth Drinker's Journal).

13. Proclamation of General Howe, November 7, 1777, Carleton Papers, Public Record Office; *Pennsylvania Evening Post,* November 8, 1777.

14. General orders of Sir William Howe, November 28, December 18, 1777, in "General Orders, September 27, 1777–February 21, 1778, of the Army in North America under General Howe," Library, Royal Artillery Institution, Woolwich, London.

15. Elizabeth to Henry Drinker, December 3, 1777, Drinker Family Papers, Quaker Manuscript Collection, Haverford College Library (hereinafter Drinker Papers).

16. *Pennsylvania Evening Post,* January 10, 1778, et seq.

17. Ibid., January 27, February 7, 1778.

18. Quoted in John F. Watson, *Annals of Philadelphia and Pennsylvania in the Olden Time,* II, 288.

19. *Pennsylvania Evening Post,* December 13, 1777.

20. General orders of Sir William Howe, February 19, 1778, Library, Royal Artillery Institution; "The Diary of Robert Morton," *PMHB* 1 (1877): October 1, 1777, pp. 10–11.

21. "The Diary of Robert Morton," *PMHB* 1 (1877): October 16, 1777, p. 19.

22. Robert Proud to William Proud, December 1, 1777, Robert Proud's Memoranda, HSP.

23. E. Morris to Samuel Neale, December 13, 1777 (copy), MS. vol. 34, Library, Friends' House, London.

24. "Diary of James Allen, Esq., of Philadelphia, Counsellor-at-Law, 1770–1778," *PMHB* 9 (1885): December 11, 1777, p. 429.

25. Anonymous intelligence report, November 17, 1777, and Jonathan Clark to George Washington, November 17, 1777, George Washington Papers, ser. 4, Library of Congress.

26. "Summary of Provisions Shipped to New York and Philadelphia as of January 15, 1779," Carleton Papers, Public Record Office. Weir had on hand in Philadelphia 1,081,184 pounds of pork, 367,290 pounds of beef, 542,416 pounds of bread, 1,642,760 pounds of flour, 99,400 pounds of butter, 9,070 pounds of peas, 284,000 pounds of oatmeal, 55,000 pounds of rice, and 126,000 gallons of rum. See Daniel Weir to Mr. Robinson, January 20, 1778 (copy), Treasury Papers, class 64, vol. 114, Public Record Office (hereinafter T. 64/114).

27. Elizabeth Drinker's Journal, January 27, 1778, p. 303.

28. Weir to Robinson, January 20, March 4, 1778, T. 64/114. Even when Weir did receive supplies, they were sometimes inedible. On one occasion he reported receiving a cargo of peas that were unfit to eat. He suspected that the damage had not occurred during shipping, but that they had been shipped in this condition. See Weir to Robinson, May 22, 1778, ibid.

29. Elizabeth Drinker's Journal, November 12, 1777, p. 301.

30. Maj. Carl Baurmeister to Maj. Gen. Friedrich Christian Arnold, freiherr von Jungkenn, January 20, 1778, *PMHB* 60 (1936): 50.

31. Proclamation of Joseph Galloway, January 22, 1778, Carleton Papers, Public Record Office.

32. Willard O. Mishoff, "Business in Philadelphia during the British Occupation, 1777–1778," *PMHB* 61 (1937): 168.

33. "Letter of Friends in Philadelphia to Friends in Ireland Soliciting Aid during the Occupation of Philadelphia by the British," and "To the Friends of Ulster and Munster, and to the Monthly-Meetings of Leinster Province," *PMHB* 20 (1896): 125–127.

34. E. Morris to Samuel Neale, December 13, 1777 (copy), MS. vol. 34, Library, Friends' House, London; Baurmeister to von Jungkenn, January 20, 1778, *PMHB* 60 (1936): 50.

35. Robert Proud to William Proud, March 1778, *PMHB* 34 (1910): 67–69.

36. "The Diary of Robert Morton," *PMHB* 1 (1877): November 27–30, 1777, pp. 31–32; *Pennsylvania Evening Post*, November 29, 1777.

37. "The Diary of Robert Morton," *PMHB* 1 (1877): December 1–3, 1777, pp. 32–33.

38. *Pennsylvania Evening Post*, November 27, 1777.

39. Brig. Gen. James Pattison to John Grant, December 21, 1777, Pattison Letterbook, Library, Royal Artillery Institution.

40. *Pennsylvania Evening Post*, November 27, 1777.

41. Mishoff, "Business in Philadelphia," p. 174; *Pennsylvania Evening Post*, December 30, 1777.

42. Elizabeth Drinker's Journal, October 6, December 18, 1777, pp. 299, 302.

43. Ibid., January 1, 1778, p. 303; Elizabeth to Henry Drinker, February 26, 1778, Drinker Papers.

44. Henry to Elizabeth Drinker, January 30, 1778, Drinker Papers.

45. Brig. Gen. James Pattison to Lord Viscount Townshend, January 22, 1778; Pattison to Brig. Gen. Cleveland, January 22, 1778; Pattison to Lord Amherst, January 23, 1778; Pattison Letterbook, Library, Royal Artillery Institution. See also Whitfield J. Bell, Jr. (ed.), "Addenda to Watson's Annals of Philadelphia: Notes by Jacob Mordecai, 1836," *PMHB* 98 (1974): 149.

46. Watson, *Annals*, II, 285, 288–289.

47. See Judith M. Diamondstone, "Philadelphia's Municipal Corporation, 1701–1776," *PMHB* 90 (1966): 183–201; and the same author's dissertation, "The Philadelphia Corporation, 1701–1776," University of Pennsylvania, 1969.

48. William Duane (ed.), *Extracts from the Diary of Christopher Marshall, 1774–1781*, October 12, 1777, p. 134 (hereinafter Christopher Marshall's Diary); proclamations of Sir William Howe, *Pennsylvania Evening Post*, October 14, 21, 1777.

49. The best recent study of Galloway's political career is Benjamin H. Newcomb, *Franklin and Galloway: A Political Partnership*. Galloway's military views are discussed in John E. Ferling, "Joseph Galloway's Military Advice: A Loyalist's View of the Revolution," *PMHB* 98 (1974): 171–188.

50. Joseph Galloway to Capt. [Robert] Mackenzie, October 25, 1777 (copy), Carleton Papers, Public Record Office.

51. Howe to Galloway, December 4, 1777, ibid. Galloway's title of superintendent of the police can cause confusion because of changes in the meaning of the term from the eighteenth to the twentieth centuries. Police forces, in anything approaching the modern sense, were at least fifty years away. There were no police*men* to superintend. Instead, in the eighteenth century, the term "to police" meant "to regulate." A policed city was a regulated city, one that had some sort of administration. Galloway's job was to govern the city, rather than simply maintain law and order, though, of course, this latter task was part of his assignment. See John M. Coleman, "Joseph Galloway and the British Occupation of Philadelphia," *Pennsylvania History* 30 (1963): 272.

52. Howe to Galloway, December 4, 1777, Carleton Papers, Public Record Office.

53. *Pennsylvania Evening Post*, December 4, 1777.

54. Ambrose Serle to Earl of Dartmouth, January 10, 1778, Dartmouth Papers, William Salt Library, Stafford, England.

55. Anne Penn to [Lady Juliana Penn], December 14, 1777, HSP; see also James H. Hutson, *Pennsylvania Politics 1746–1770: The Movement for Royal Government and Its Consequences.*

56. Coleman, "Joseph Galloway and the British Occupation of Philadelphia," p. 279.

57. *The Narrative of Lieut. Gen. Sir William Howe, in a Committee of the House of Commons . . . Letters to A Nobleman,* pp. 41–44.

58. Ibid., pp. 41–42.

59. *Pennsylvania Evening Post*, December 9, 1777, January 8, 1778.

60. Proclamation of Joseph Galloway, *Pennsylvania Evening Post*, January 15, 1778; original in Carleton Papers, Public Record Office. On the eve of the Revolution, Philadelphians were very conscious of the appearance and cleanliness of their city. See Charles S. Olton, "Philadelphia's First Environmental Crisis," *PMHB* 98 (1974): 90–100.

61. Proclamation of Joseph Galloway, *Pennsylvania Evening Post*, March 23, 1778; original in Carleton Papers, Public Record Office.

62. Ibid., January 15, 1778.

63. Ibid., January 22, 1778.

64. Ibid., February 12, 1778.

65. *Pennsylvania Evening Post*, November 1, 1777.

66. Ambrose Serle to Earl of Dartmouth, January 10, 1778, Dartmouth Papers, Salt Library.

67. Mishoff, "Business in Philadelphia," p. 167; Christopher Marshall's Diary, February 27, 1778, p. 169. By February, there were reportedly 121 new stores kept by English, Irish, Scottish, and American merchants.

68. Frederick Lewis Pattee, "The British Theater in Philadelphia in 1778," *American Literature* 6 (1935): 381–388.

69. Christopher Marshall's Diary, December 28, 1777, p. 152.

70. Philadelphia Meeting for Suffering to London Meeting, February 26, 1778, "Letters to and from Philadelphia," vol. 1, Library, Friends' House, London.

71. Seybolt, "Contemporary British Account," p. 83.

72. Letter from Captain Hinrichs, On the Neck Near Philadelphia, January 18, 1778, in *Letters from America 1776–1779, Being Letters of Brunswick, Hessian, and Waldeck Officers with the British Armies during the Revolution,* trans. Ray W. Pettengill, pp. 182–187.

73. Letter from Captain Hinrichs, June 2, 1778, ibid., pp. 188–190.

74. Watson, *Annals*, II, 288.

75. J. Thomas Scharf and Thompson Westcott, *History of Philadelphia 1609–1884*, I, 384.

76. Gruber, *Howe Brothers*, p. 280; Alden, *American Revolution*, pp. 197, 200.

77. Memorandum of Thomas Willing, November 2, 1777, Thomas Willing Papers, HSP.

78. Howe to Germain, October 22, 1777 (extract), Carleton Papers, Public Record Office.

79. The term was derived from two Italian words, *mescere*, to mix, and *mischiare*, to mingle (Watson, *Annals*, III, 471).

80. Elizabeth Drinker's Journal, May 18, 1778, p. 306; Baurmeister to von Jungkenn, June 15, 1778, *PMHB* 60 (1936): 179–180; Watson, *Annals*, II, 290–292.

81. Elizabeth Drinker's Journal, May 18, 1778, p. 306; Edward H. Tatum, Jr. (ed.), *The American Journal of Ambrose Serle, Secretary to Lord Howe 1776–1778*, p. 294.

82. Baurmeister to von Jungkenn, May 10, 1778, *PMHB* 60 (1936): 171–172.

83. William Eden to Alexander Wedderburn (?), June 5, 1778, Auckland Papers (Additional Manuscripts 46491), British Museum.

84. Testimony of Maj. Gen. Grey before the House of Commons, May 6, 1779, State Papers, Domestic, George III, vol. 37, no. 18, Public Record Office; quotation of John Potts in Wallace Brown, *The Good Americans: The Loyalists in the American Revolution*, p. 61.

85. Joseph Galloway (New York) to Ambrose Serle (London), July 13, 1778, enclosed in Serle to Earl of Dartmouth, September 16, 1778, Dartmouth Papers, Salt Library.

86. Daniel Weir to Mr. Robinson, June 15, 1778, T. 64/114; Elizabeth Drinker's Journal, June 16, 1778, p. 307.

87. Elizabeth Drinker's Journal, June 16, 1778, p. 307; *Diary of Grace Growden Galloway*, June 17, 1778, p. 36.

88. Elizabeth Drinker's Journal, June 18, 1778, p. 307.

89. *Pennsylvania Evening Post*, June 20, 1778.

90. Elizabeth Drinker's Journal, June 2, 4, 1778, p. 308.

91. John Shy, "The American Revolution: The Military Conflict Considered as a Revolutionary War," in *Essays on the American Revolution*, ed. Stephen G. Kurtz and James H. Hutson, p. 147.

BIBLIOGRAPHY

Manuscript Material

England:
  British Museum, London
    Auckland Papers
  Friends' House, London
    Letters to and from Philadelphia, vol. 1
    MS. vol. 34
  Public Record Office, London
    Carleton Papers
    Colonial Office Papers, class 5
    State Papers, Domestic, George III
    Treasury Papers, class 64
  Royal Artillery Institution, Woolwich, London
    General Orders, September 27, 1777–February 21,
      1778, of the Army in North America under General Howe
    Letterbook of Brig. Gen. James Pattison
  William Salt Library, Stafford
    Dartmouth Papers
United States:
  Haverford College Library, Haverford, Pennsylvania
    Drinker Family Papers
  Historical Society of Pennsylvania, Philadelphia
    Penn Papers
    Robert Proud's Memoranda
    Thomas Willing Papers
  Library of Congress, Washington, D.C.
    George Washington Papers

Published Material

Alden, John Richard. *The American Revolution, 1775–1783.* New York: Harper and Row, 1954.

Anderson, Troyer Steele. *The Command of the Howe Brothers dur-*

ing the American Revolution. New York: Oxford University Press, 1936.

Bell, Whitfield J., Jr., ed. "Addenda to Watson's Annals of Philadelphia: Notes by Jacob Mordecai, 1836." *Pennsylvania Magazine of History and Biography* 98 (1974): 131–170.

Brown, Wallace. *The Good Americans: The Loyalists in the American Revolution.* New York: William Morrow and Co., 1969.

Coleman, John M. "Joseph Galloway and the British Occupation of Philadelphia." *Pennsylvania History* 30 (1963): 272–300.

Diamondstone, Judith M. "Philadelphia's Municipal Corporation, 1701–1776." *Pennsylvania Magazine of History and Biography* 90 (1966): 183–201.

Diary of Grace Growden Galloway. New York: New York Times and Arno Press, 1971.

"Diary of James Allen, Esq., of Philadelphia, Counsellor-at-Law, 1770–1778." *Pennsylvania Magazine of History and Biography* 9 (1885): 176–196, 278–296, 424–441.

"The Diary of Robert Morton." *Pennsylvania Magazine of History and Biography* 1 (1877): 1–39.

Duane, William, ed. *Extracts from the Diary of Christopher Marshall, 1774–1781.* New York: New York Times and Arno Press, 1969.

"Extracts from the Journal of Mrs. Henry Drinker, of Philadelphia, from September 25, 1777, to July 4, 1778." *Pennsylvania Magazine of History and Biography* 13 (1889): 298–308.

Ferling, John E. "Joseph Galloway's Military Advice: A Loyalist's View of the Revolution." *Pennsylvania Magazine of History and Biography* 98 (1974): 171–188.

[Galloway, Joseph]. *Letters to a Nobleman on the Conduct of the War in the Middle Colonies.* 3d ed. London: J. Wilkie, 1780.

Gruber, Ira D. *The Howe Brothers and the American Revolution.* New York: Atheneum, 1972.

Hutson, James H. *Pennsylvania Politics 1746–1770: The Movement for Royal Government and Its Consequences.* Princeton: Princeton University Press, 1972.

"Letter of Friends in Philadelphia to Friends in Ireland Soliciting Aid during the Occupation of Philadelphia by the British." *Pennsylvania Magazine of History and Biography* 20 (1896): 125–126.

Mishoff, Willard O. "Business in Philadelphia during the British Occupation, 1777–1778." *Pennsylvania Magazine of History and Biography* 61 (1937): 165–181.

The Narrative of Lieut. Gen. Sir William Howe, in a Committee of the House of Commons . . . Letters to A Nobleman. 3d ed. London: H. Baldwin, 1781.

Newcomb, Benjamin H. *Franklin and Galloway: A Political Partnership.* New Haven: Yale University Press, 1972.

Oaks, Robert F. "Philadelphians in Exile: The Problem of Loyalty during the American Revolution." *Pennsylvania Magazine of History and Biography* 96 (1972): 298–325.

Olton, Charles S. "Philadelphia's First Environmental Crisis." *Pennsylvania Magazine of History and Biography* 98 (1974): 90–100.

Pattee, Frederick Lewis. "The British Theater in Philadelphia in 1778." *American Literature* 6 (1935): 381–388.

Pennsylvania Evening Post, 1777–1778.

Pettengill, Ray W., trans. *Letters from America 1776–1779, Being Letters of Brunswick, Hessian, and Waldeck Officers with the British Armies during the Revolution.* Boston and New York: Houghton Mifflin Co., 1924.

Scharf, J. Thomas, and Thompson Westcott. *History of Philadelphia, 1609–1884.* 3 vols. Philadelphia: L. H. Everts and Co., 1884.

Scull, G. D., ed. "Journal of Captain John Montresor, July 1, 1777, to July 1, 1778, Chief Engineer of the British Army." *Pennsylvania Magazine of History and Biography* 6 (1882): 34–57, 189–206, 284–299.

Seybolt, Robert Francis. "A Contemporary British Account of General Sir William Howe's Military Operations in 1777." *American Antiquarian Society Proceedings,* n.s., 40 (1930): 69–92.

Shy, John. "The American Revolution: The Military Conflict Considered as a Revolutionary War." In *Essays on the American Revo-*

lution, edited by Stephen G. Kurtz and James H. Hutson. Chapel
Hill: Published for the Institute of Early American History and
Culture by the University of North Carolina Press, 1973.

Stevens, Benjamin Franklin, ed. *Facsimiles of Manuscripts in European Archives Relating to America, 1773–1783*. 25 vols. London:
C. Whittingham and Co., 1889–1895.

Tatum, Edward H., Jr., ed. *The American Journal of Ambrose Serle,
Secretary to Lord Howe 1776–1778*. San Marino: Huntington Library, 1940.

"To the Friends of Ulster and Munster, and to the Monthly-Meetings of Leinster Province." *Pennsylvania Magazine of History and
Biography* 20 (1896): 126–127.

Warner, Sam Bass, Jr. *The Private City: Philadelphia in Three Periods of Its Growth*. Philadelphia: University of Pennsylvania Press,
1968.

Watson, John F. *Annals of Philadelphia and Pennsylvania in the
Olden Time*. 3 vols. Philadelphia: Edwin S. Stuart, 1898–1905.

Urban Response to Jacksonian Democracy:
Philadelphia Democrats and the Bank War, 1832–1834

BY BRUCE I. AMBACHER

DURING THE ADMINISTRATION of Andrew Jackson, no issue created greater social, cultural, economic, and political repercussions for the Democrats of Philadelphia than that of President Jackson's attack on the Second Bank of the United States. Since the Bank was headquartered in Philadelphia and had widespread support, the response of city Democrats to this issue was crucial to the outcome of the Bank War. Between 1832 and 1834 this struggle shook, split, reshaped, and reunited political parties as politicians fought on national, state, and local levels, in the newspapers, at mass meetings, on the campaign stump, through the ballot, and through the money box. The vehemence of their rhetoric and their actions escalated and climaxed with political bloodshed and death.

Historians have viewed the Bank War as a sectional struggle between the urban northeast and the rural south and west, an economic contest between agrarianism and industrialism, a hard money crusade, or a raw political contest. The latter interpretation most aptly describes the motivations behind the Bank War in Philadelphia.[1]

The Democratic party that emerged in the city from this contest clearly demonstrated the impact of the restructuring of the two-party system and of local subservience to the views, rhetoric, and leadership of the national party. The war accelerated the shifting of city Democratic leadership from the established patrician leaders who had been powerful before Andrew Jackson to the younger, mass-, and patronage-oriented leaders who emerged into positions of control by 1834.[2] This shift reflected the impact of not only the Bank War but also the ever-broadening participation of the common man in economic and political life. The emergence of the sans-culottes as a political factor required leaders able to understand and shape the masses. Generally of a lower social standing and occupational status than the "old guard," these "patronage partisans" willingly followed the national leadership and echoed the themes of class struggle and "monster monopoly" seen so frequently in the *Washington Globe*, the party's national organ.

The Bank War also influenced political methods and tactics. Although the involvement of the rank and file of the party's membership in political rallies and petition campaigns was not unprecedented by 1832, the greater scope and frequency of their use during the Bank War was an innovation often attributed to the antislavery movement. For the first time as well, the masses that elected Andrew Jackson in 1828 were being unleashed against an issue, an idea. The mass party existed. To keep it busy, it was turned against the "monster monopoly." The use of such masses in such ways was peculiarly urban, a factor frequently ignored or minimized in accounts of the Bank War. In Pennsylvania, only the urban southeastern part surrounding Philadelphia was caught up in the furor over the Bank. Contemporary politicians acknowledged that the rural areas remained firmly Jacksonian.[3]

Finally, the Bank War reshaped the Democratic party in Philadelphia because the national issues both supplanted and blended with local issues on an unprecedented scale. The questions of the Bank's recharter and its relationship to the federal government became the major issues in the political debates and battles in the city.

Late in 1831 the position of the Second Bank of the United States appeared secure in Philadelphia and throughout the nation. Its charter would not expire for another five years, and, although President Jackson personally opposed the Bank and its recharter, the Democratic party was not sufficiently united for him to make his view party gospel. His recent statements on the Bank demonstrated moderation and an apparent willingness to defer to the wishes of Congress in favor of recharter.[4]

Although Philadelphia Democrats openly supported the Bank for its past benefits to the government and the economy, most were extremely cautious in their support of early recharter. In 1832 they pursued every effort to postpone such a move or to secure an administration compromise to avoid being forced to publicly choose between Jackson and the Bank. They wanted the Bank but believed the nation "would continue to exist without it."[5]

Democrats in Philadelphia and Washington were correct in their assumption that the early recharter movement was at least partially politically motivated. Bank President Nicholas Biddle's request for recharter in January 1832 consciously made it part of the presidential campaign, since the National Republican candidates, Henry Clay and John Sergeant, were both on the Bank's payroll. Biddle's choice of congressional sponsors, Senator George M. Dallas of Philadelphia and Representative George

McDuffie of South Carolina, viewed by Biddle as pro-Bank Democrats, reflected his intention to force Democrats to choose between Jackson and the Bank or to secure a compromise. The course of the recharter bill through Congress, the House investigation into its past conduct, and the vote for recharter affirmed the political nature of the issue.[6]

On the tenth of July 1832, President Jackson vetoed the recharter bill. Intended more for the public than for Congress, his veto message focused on the Bank's monopoly privileges and the undesirable potential represented by the large bloc of foreign stockholders. He also doubted the Bank's constitutionality, despite the Supreme Court's position in McCulloch vs. Maryland, and claimed that the recharter represented another effort by the "rich and powerful" to "bend the acts of government to their selfish purposes."[7]

The veto, and the Senate's failure to override it, came as no surprise to politicians in Philadelphia, but they were divided over how to respond to its potential impact on the 1832 elections. The old-guard "silk-stocking" Democrats, whose editorial voice was State Assemblyman Peter Hay's *American Sentinel*, at first counseled caution and moderation. Led by federal officeholders, the patronage Democrats expanded their new weekly newspaper into a daily. The *Pennsylvanian*, edited by Benjamin Mifflin, quickly became the dominant voice of local Democrats who supported Jackson and the veto.[8]

But a minority of "original" Jacksonians, whose principal organ was the *Pennsylvania Inquirer*, controlled by Robert Morris and Jesper Harding, left the Democratic party with "deep regret and mortification." They saw the choice facing Philadelphia Democrats as "Jackson or the Bank," and they chose the latter.[9] Other pro-Bank newspapers raged against the veto and labeled it a manifesto against the entire federal structure. They counterattacked by stressing the benefits of the Bank for the currency, the economy, and city business and labor.[10]

The most decisive action by the antiveto elements came on July 16, 1832, with a mass rally in Independence Square to denounce the veto and Jackson. Defecting original Jacksonians formed a large share of the meeting's officers. One loyal Jacksonian characterized the officers as "apostate Jacksonians, Federalists, and disappointed office seekers." This rally marked the first time either political elite turned to their supporters in an attempt to influence public opinion. Contemporary estimates of the crowd (1,500 to 8,000) seemed quite impressive compared to previous town-meeting crowds of only a few hundred.[11]

Inspired (or frightened) by the antiveto rally and possible further defections in the city, the various Democratic factions began to organize a "Jackson—Bank or no Bank" rally for the same site one week later. The editors of both Democratic newspapers, over thirty officeholders, and virtually every prominent Democrat in the city and county signed the announcement of this rally.[12]

The rally began with bands leading marching Democrats, "the bone and sinew" of the party, from the various wards into Independence Square. This time, estimates of the crowd went as high as twenty thousand, with the Democrats labeling it the largest rally ever held in Philadelphia.

Congressman Henry Horn, unanimously elected president of the rally, demonstrated the political expediency of many Democrats in his opening speech. He explained away his earlier vote to recharter the Bank as being directed by the opinions and sentiments of his constituents, not his own conscience. Senator Dallas, in a similar address, praised General Jackson and concentrated on the accomplishments of his first term, but *"He did not utter a syllable with reference to the Bank."* Charles J. Ingersoll, who five months earlier had labored as Nicholas Biddle's agent in an unsuccessful effort to secure an administration-sponsored compromise recharter bill, spoke along this same line— "not *against* the Bank, but for General Jackson."

Postmaster James Page presented the resolutions, which the meeting adopted unanimously. They praised the president for his "defense of the people against odious and dangerous monopolies," condemned the Bank for tying recharter to the presidential campaign, and supported Jackson, "*Bank or no Bank.*" Indeed, if the issue was drawn, their "course must be—*Jackson and no Bank.*"[13]

Bank supporters had a field day dwelling on the cost of the rally (estimated by one to have exceeded $1,000) and on the inconsistencies of those Democrats who voted for recharter and then addressed the rally. The *National Gazette* observed that "there is no stronger example of 'kissing the rod.' Men often 'eat their words' from necessity or cupidity, but it is a rather new thing to eat legislative votes."[14]

Pro-Bank Democrats who attended this rally chose partisanship over principle and, in effect, pledged eternal homage to Jackson and expediency in return for the anticipated rewards of victory at the polls. Although the "patronage partisans" would lead the struggle against the Bank, the decision of the moderate and pro-Bank Democrats to support this crusade ensured its success. They determined the political outcome of the Bank War in Philadelphia. Nicholas Biddle thus failed to separate pro-Bank Democrats from Jackson. Instead, he separated them from the Bank.

Throughout the autumn of 1832, politicians and their partisan newspapers poured out a continuous stream of rhetoric. The anti-Jackson coalition concentrated on the dictatorial stance assumed by Jackson and asked the voters to defeat him, thereby ending his mockery of the courts, Congress, and the Constitution. Another theme made the Bank the victim of a New York–Pennsylvania rivalry. Jackson's opponents claimed that recharter had been vetoed so a new bank could be located in New York City. There it would be subservient to Wall Street and to Martin Van Buren, the national Jacksonian vice-presidential candidate so widely disliked by commonwealth politicians of all persuasions. Bank supporters coupled Jackson's opposition to the Bank with his opposition to tariff protection and internal improvements, which the state favored. They also mocked the duplicity and disaffection of Jacksonians in the state congressional delegation who had first supported the Bank and other Pennsylvania measures, then abandoned them after the veto. The opposition press labeled them "collar" Democrats because they bowed their necks to the yoke of Jackson's dictates and political expediency. Finally, these politicians called the Bank veto the "doctrine of nullification in its worst form," since it left all officials free to interpret the Constitution for themselves.[15]

To offset the negative impact and criticism of the veto in Philadelphia, city Democrats struck back. At first they reiterated the veto themes of monopoly, foreign control, class conflict, and antirepublicanism. They also quickly cracked the whip of party discipline to force pro-Bank Democrats to explain and justify their past votes and to show proper support for Jackson against the Bank in the future in order to remain in the party. A final Democratic theme depicted the Bank as an evil election machine that dominated and corrupted the free electoral process. Its destruction would preserve free government. Even if the Bank had once been useful, it had gone beyond the objects for which it was established and sought to control the voters and the political institutions of the nation. The loss of the first minor elections of 1832 reaffirmed the Democratic belief that the "MAMMOTH BANK," headquartered in the city, was opening its vaults to corrupt the voters.[16]

As the state and congressional campaigns drew to a close, both sides focused their rhetoric on the single theme of Andrew Jackson: Would the president of the United States or the Bank of the United States be vindicated and rule the nation? Both sides felt there was no neutral course.[17]

Philadelphia went to the polls on Tuesday, October 9, 1832, a wet and dreary day in the city. Party workers began pasting up handbills at 4:00 A.M. The polls opened at 8:30 A.M. and did not close until 10:00 that evening. Some observers reported an increased number of fistfights between partisans. The city returns went anti-Jacksonian, while the more Democratic county vote produced significantly reduced Jacksonian majorities. On a combined city-county basis, the Democrats trailed by over 4,700 votes. One important but generally unperceived effect of this virtually complete defeat of traditional Democrats was the increased use of the younger "patronage partisans" as candidates in later contests.[18]

In the gubernatorial race, Democratic Governor George Wolf's slender 313-vote majority in the county failed to offset antimasonic contender Joseph Ritner's 1,400-vote lead in the city. Statewide, the race remained in doubt for two weeks. Wolf's 1,832 majority, a slim 50.85 percent of the vote, compared quite unfavorably with his 60 percent majority three years earlier.[19]

The anti-Jacksonians surveyed the city-county vote for the rest of the local contests with great pleasure: They had elected two of the four congressmen, the state senator, six of the eight state assemblymen, the Common and Select councils, the sheriff, the auditor, and the county commissioner. They also took special pleasure in the defeat of the only Pennsylvania congressman to vote against the Bank from York County.[20]

In view of the sweep of the state elections, the anti-Jacksonian campaign during the month between those elections and the presidential balloting showed surprising caution and doubt. Bank supporters boasted, of course, that the gubernatorial results made it clear that Pennsylvania would vote against Jackson. They also spread the rumor that Jackson intended to remove the government deposits from the Bank after his reelection. Finally, they labeled as a smokescreen Democratic assertions and resolutions charging the Bank with interference in the elections to divert attention from the real issues delineated throughout the fall.[21]

Democrats publicly rationalized their earlier defeat and blamed it on *"the corruption engendered and fed by the Bank."* Ward meetings passed resolutions reaffirming Democratic faith in Jackson and the veto, and condemning the Bank as the *"hydra-* headed monster" of corruption. The *Pennsylvanian* saw the contest, now more than ever, as one "between the United States Bank with two hundred millions at its command, and the American people." Privately, a few leaders admitted that "unwise management" by some newer Democratic leaders and national interference in local politics had been partially to blame for their earlier defeat.[22]

Twenty thousand fewer Pennsylvanians went to the polls in November 1832 than had voted the previous month. Democrats attributed this to pro-Bank disillusionment over the failure to defeat Wolf and the growing realization they could not defeat Jackson. The president received only 45.7 percent of the city-county vote compared to 66.5 percent in 1828. Statewide, he polled 57.6 percent compared to 66.6 percent four years earlier. Clearly, the Bank issue hurt Jackson not only in the city but also across the state.[23]

For most Democrats across the nation, the Bank War ended with Jackson's vindication by reelection. But this was not the case for Democrats in Philadelphia. Jackson now viewed the election as a mandate to cripple the Bank. To accomplish this, he needed evidence that could be supplied only by the government directors of the Bank. For the first time these positions would be important. Throughout December the administration conferred with Philadelphia Democrats regarding suitable appointments. Lists of candidates, their qualifications, and their willingness to serve circulated between Philadelphia and Washington. Most who declined to serve shared the view of one former director, who informed Jackson that "it would require months of close investigation to come to any just knowledge" of the Bank's affairs.[24] Most politicians did not want to devote that time to invisible activity.

The administration reappointed three dependable Democrats and named two new ones for 1833. The most effective of the appointees, Henry D. Gilpin, had been federal district attorney in Philadelphia for more than a year. The most controversial, Peter Wager, reflected the impact of the Bank War upon political leadership in the city. Established Democrats detested Wager and his style and blamed his appointment on the Kitchen Cabinet. Regardless of their differences, all were Democrats devoted to curtailing the Bank.[25]

These government directors demonstrated a new spirit of independence at the first meeting of the Bank's board of directors in 1833 to elect the president and appoint the committees for the year. They cast blank ballots rather than vote for Biddle. Biddle, serving for the first time as a private director, became the first president of the Bank elected by a minority of the board and without government endorsement. Biddle responded to this insult by excluding the government directors from all key committees and by ignoring crucial matters during full board meetings. Following this initial skirmish, the government directors settled in to attend board meetings, learn the intricacies of national banking, and use their position to gather information for Jackson's further assaults upon the Bank.[26]

During the early spring, members of the administration debated whether to use evidence from various sources to prepare a legal suit to break the Bank's charter. They finally persuaded Jackson that he lacked sufficient evidence to sustain such a suit. He leaned more toward removal of the government deposits and instructed the government directors to gather the necessary evidence.[27]

Jackson's first informal request to the government directors for evidence brought a negative response. They viewed his action as premature and feared that any investigation not sanctioned by the secretary of the treasury would be "repelled with prompt distrust" and would be defeated. Jackson, not yet ready to proceed formally, delayed action.[28]

The public campaign to make removal an acceptable political act in Philadelphia soon began. Just two days after President Jackson recommended removal to his cabinet, the *Pennsylvanian* called upon the administration to withdraw the deposits. Subsequent editorials justified this policy with most of the same arguments Old Hickory had presented to his cabinet.[29]

In early May 1833, Jackson effected cabinet changes designed to facilitate removal. Jackson knew of Secretary of the Treasury Louis McLane's reluctance to order removal and elevated him to the State Department. William Duane, Jr., of Philadelphia became the new secretary of the treasury. Jackson was aware of Duane's hostility to the Bank but not of his opposition to removal.

City Democrats also concentrated on political fence-mending and party unity to build a political climate favorable to removal. Jackson's visit to the city, as part of a northern tour to capitalize upon his increased popularity after curbing the nullification threat, provided the opportunity to demonstrate party unity. Jacksonians of all persuasions joined in the planning, reception, and feting of Old Hickory in early June. The visit brought out a display of unity and a respite from the Bank controversy; there appears to have been no public or private discussion of the Bank with Jackson.[30]

The next month when Democrats celebrated the anniversary of American independence, the vast majority of the party attended the "UNION AND HARMONY GRAND DEMOCRATIC FESTIVAL" presided over by former Senator Dallas. Dallas's remarks focused on the democratic principles of the Declaration of Independence and the Constitution and their fulfillment in the War of 1812 (climaxed by Old Hickory's victory at New Orleans) and Jackson's Force Bill of March 1833, respectively. He closed by urging all citizens to support the Democratic party, the party most congenial with the principles and institutions of the Union.

Postmaster James Page, in behalf of the "Young Democrats," presided over the only rival Democratic celebration. Two Democrats there offered the only anti-Bank toasts of the day. Most Democrats appeared unwilling to muddy the political waters regarding the Bank and seemed uncertain about the proper course to follow. They waited for the administration to act.[31]

In late July, Special Treasury Agent Amos Kendall began a tour of state banks to determine which might receive the government deposits. Although no decision had yet been made on removal, Democrats in Philadelphia asserted that Kendall had been appointed to arrange for transferring funds after Jackson ordered that step.[32]

Both Democratic papers followed Kendall's mission from city to city and quickly reported overwhelming success in Philadelphia. Within two days four banks indicated a willingness to handle the deposits. Others, also favorably disposed, sought authorization from their boards of directors.[33]

While politicians and their partisan presses argued the merits and legalities of removing the deposits, Jackson renewed his efforts to obtain evidence for a suit against the Bank from the government directors. He requested an examination of the Bank president's expense account. Biddle reluctantly complied with the request for his books. When the government directors questioned Biddle on certain items, especially an unitemized $80,000 entry for preparation, printing, and circulation of documents, he refused to give any explanation. Although surprised and shaken by the disclosures, the private board members nonetheless supported Biddle's refusal and voted their confidence in his use of the funds. Both Kendall and Jackson believed these unitemized expenses justified their determination to remove the deposits.[34]

During the next several weeks Democratic presses editorialized for removal. When Jackson announced that removal would begin in October 1833, these papers called the decision the preservation of democracy, a "New Orleans victory" over the aristocracy, a *coup de grâce*, and a fulfillment of the veto.[35]

Pro-Bank forces exploded against removal with nearly as much fury as they had expended against the veto. They charged Jackson with disregarding his cabinet, mocking Congress, and defying the law. They denied that the election of 1832 was a mandate to crush the Bank. Bank supporters also denied the damaging Democratic charge that the Bank had bribed newspapers.[36]

Following these initial outbursts of rather obligatory support or condemnation, both parties began efforts to translate their sentiments into the only terms that counted—majorities at the polls. The October 1833 city elections became a vote of confidence for or against Jackson and removal. "Perhaps there never was a city election—a mere local election," wrote one Jacksonian paper, "that engrossed the attention of the whole country in a greater degree, than the approaching contest in the city and county of Philadelphia." Anti-Jacksonians asserted that any reduction in their majorities of 1832 "would be hailed by the enemy as *recovery* of dominance in our city" and proof that Philadelphians sanctioned removal.[37]

The *American Sentinel*, which had hung back thus far in the Bank War, tried to remove that question from the city elections. Democratic candidates had been selected without reference to the Bank, it asserted, and would never have to decide about it. Furthermore, the "great mass of the democratic voters are perfectly indifferent on the question and do not wish to agitate it." If Bank supporters drew the line in this contest between "*Democracy or the Bank*," it predicted, all true Democrats would vote "*Huzza for Democracy and down with the Bank*."[38]

As the election approached, Democrats supplemented their attack on the Bank with greater attention to local issues. They gave increased space to differences over the interpretation and execution of Stephen Girard's will, the control and operation of the city waterworks, the operation of the city council, and the Hicksite controversy within the Society of Friends.[39]

The 1833 city election returns showed dramatic Democratic gains. In the county the party regained the state assembly and state senate seats by 1,800-vote margins. Although they still lost in the city, the shift in votes was just as dramatic. Joel B. Sutherland defeated a Bank lawyer and director, John Sergeant, in a special election in the first congressional district. His victory was hailed as proof that Philadelphians accepted removal.[40]

As 1833 closed, both sides in Philadelphia focused on the last phase of the Bank War—the economic pressure caused by the Bank's restriction of loans. Bank supporters admitted "unparalleled" pressure in the money market but blamed the situation on Jackson's abuse of executive power. They called for restoration of the deposits and recharter of the Bank as the only remedy. Most Democrats denied that removal caused the pressure.

All factions looked for decisive action from Congress as the only solution.[41]

In this final phase of the war both sides returned to the manipulation of public opinion through mass rallies and petitions as a tactic to gain victory. Again the anti-Jacksonians initiated the action while the Democrats copied and improved these tactics.

On the last day of 1833, a pro-Bank town meeting passed resolutions highlighting the economic pressure and calling for restoration of the deposits as the only means of relief. Democrats complained that the organizers of the meeting had broken their pledge not to bring up anything related to the Bank.[42]

Early in January 1834, Biddle pressured many city banks to withdraw standing offers to handle the government deposits and to sign a bankers' memorial for the restoration of those deposits to his Bank. Bank supporters made it appear that only the Girard Bank, the "pet" bank of the city, refused to sign the memorial, while Democrats correctly insisted that six other banks also refused.[43]

Similar antiremoval memorials, resolutions, and meetings held throughout February rallied public opinion, kept sentiments high, and influenced Congress. The "Memorial of Manufacturers, Mechanics, Merchants, Traders, and Others" for the restoration of the deposits, signed by 108,000 people, was the largest petition transmitted to President Jackson and Congress. Jackson, of course, refused to yield and in a contrived rage told the delegation to go home and look to Mr. Biddle and his Bank for relief, since he, not Jackson, was responsible for the economic pressure.[44]

Democrats used their Battle of New Orleans Day celebration on January 8, 1834, to counterattack. "Volunteer" toasts from the Democratic ranks showed a marked increase in anti-Bank sentiment in both number and feeling. Democratic ward, district, and town meetings in late January and early February provided a second means of vocalizing the growing anti-Bank sentiment. The meetings passed resolutions praising the president's actions against the Bank and reconfirming their opposition to recharter.[45]

The most crucial test of Philadelphia Democrats' commitment to Jacksonian banking policy came in late January when the economic pressure forced postponement of payments on the state loans. Pro-Bank forces expected Governor Wolf and the state Democrats to side with the Bank and call for the restoration of the deposits in order to win Bank support for the state loan payments. Instead, Wolf placed full blame for the problem on Bank efforts to coerce recharter from the federal government.[46]

Even before Wolf's message to the legislature, city Democrats had planned the largest public rally yet held in Independence Square. Wolf's message permitted them to take a more openly anti-Bank stance in the speeches and resolutions. Over fifteen thousand Democrats jammed the square to attend the March 4, 1834, rally presided over by Attorney General Dallas. In his opening remarks, Dallas concentrated on the need for Democratic unity to continue the party's opposition to the Bank.

Dallas then offered resolutions he had written, which blamed the Bank and the paper-money system for the economic distress. Praising Wolf and his Democratic supporters, Dallas also called upon Congress to sell its stock in the Bank. Following the usual unanimous adoption of the resolutions, former Congressman Charles J. Ingersoll and former Secretary of the Treasury Richard Rush "spoke at length and in the most animated manner" against the Bank.[47]

The Whig Powelton Jubilee on April 22, 1834, proved to be the climax of the anti-Jacksonian spring propaganda and

public opinion. Announcements of the rally and picnic to cele-
brate the New York City election returns used the term "Whig"
for the first time to denote the anti-Jacksonian elements in
Philadelphia. It came into common usage quickly. In order to
maximize attendance, Whig merchants closed their shops, the
owners of the Market Street Bridge exempted those attending
the celebration from the toll, and the sponsors made the jubilee
free. The Whigs claimed sixty thousand people from Pennsylvania, New York, New Jersey, and Delaware came to eat, drink,
and be harangued by prominent Whigs, who called the celebration overwhelming proof of the growing anti-Jacksonian sentiment. Democrats regarded it as proof of what lavish spending
and the lure of free food could do and bitterly criticized the
electioneering tactics used, probably because they could not respond in kind.[48]

Democrats used two incidents in mid-1834 to offset the
Powelton Jubilee and to reemphasize their conviction that the
Bank was a threat to democracy and the national economy. In
May Bank directors refused to submit to a Congressional investigation of its loans. Biddle called the attempt an unconstitu-
tional and unreasonable search and seizure. Jacksonians labeled
the refusal bold arrogance, an irresponsible error, and the
crowning blow to the grand mistake of the monopoly. They
exulted that "bankism totters in the city of Philadelphia."[49]
Biddle's refusal to submit further reduced public support for
the Bank.

The second, much more serious event alienated all but the
staunchest Bank supporters. Widely published correspondence
between Biddle and a committee of New York merchants revealed that the Bank had manufactured and manipulated the
economic pressure of the preceding months to force recharter
and restoration of the deposits, just as the Democrats had
charged. When that failed, Biddle responded to numerous pleas

and agreed to meet "the extraordinary demand" for assistance by extending nearly ten million dollars in new credit. Whig presses printed the story with little comment, while Democratic papers charged that it proved what they had been saying all along and wondered when Biddle would strike again.[50]

The highlight of Philadelphia's Democratic campaign against the Bank in 1834 came in its Fourth of July celebration. The events of the winter and spring had been capped by Democratic victories in the Southwark district constable election in May. Democrats across the state and nation realized that a massive display of party unity could tip public opinion and votes in the city and county in their favor.[51]

George M. Dallas again presided over the festivities on the fourth. The orator of the day was Henry D. Gilpin, whose renomination as a government director for 1834 had been twice defeated by the Bank-influenced Senate. Former Congressman Henry Horn, also rejected by the Senate as a government director, read the Declaration of Independence. The guests of the day included the biggest names of the Bank War.

In his keynote address Gilpin denounced the Bank and its coalition with the emerging Whig party. He pledged continuing support for Jackson and called upon the audience to sustain the party against the Bank and nullification. Both the resolutions and the toasts reflected these themes.[52]

Throughout the fall campaign, Democrats delineated each contest in a Bank–anti-Bank framework. They grew quite optimistic regarding their prospects. Some indulged dreams of victory in the city. Others confidently expected success in the combined city-county delegation to the state legislature.[53]

Philadelphia's young Whigs feared continued identification with the Bank, in light of the current shifts in public opinion, would harm their party. At a mid-September city-wide caucus they adopted resolutions "positively disclaiming any connexion with the United States Bank, or any other Bank! !" But it was too little, too late.[54]

The campaign grew so bitter and heated that both sides predicted (or feared) violence at the polls. Democrats warned that Whig decisions to close shops on election day to permit their workers to vote would lead to large concentrations of idle partisans and could result in violence.[55] Unfortunately, both the contest for ward election inspectors and the general election produced bloodshed.

As William Perry stood in line to vote at Locust Ward on the night of October 2, 1834, a scuffle flared up between Whigs and Democrats across the street. The crowd dispersed and a large group ran past the Democratic voting line. Suddenly someone stabbed Perry in the groin. He slumped, groaned, and asked for help. Following emergency surgery, he was carried home, where he died. More than four thousand Democrats attended his funeral and contributed to a fund for a monument in Locust Ward. The state offered a $600 reward but never apprehended a suspect.

Jacksonians blamed the murder on the repeated Whig cries for blood and revolution and on the closing of Whig shops on election day. They also pointed out that other Democrats had been stabbed in Spring Garden and Southwark wards.[56]

Violence broke out again in the general elections on October 14, 1834. Whigs in Moyamensing Ward drove Democrats from the polls with musketfire and tore down their election head-quarters tent and hickory pole. Later that night Democratic re-inforcements from Southwark, Northern Liberties, and Spring Garden wards assembled in Moyamensing and rushed the Whig headquarters. Musketfire from the house wounded twenty and killed James Bath. A second Democratic rush forced the Whigs to flee. Democrats then took the furniture from the house, piled it around the Whig liberty pole (which had been strapped with iron so it could not be cut down), and set it afire. The flames spread to the house and then to the entire row of four homes. Firemen were stoned and prevented from putting out the fire.

Both sides blamed the other for the violence and murder. Democrats pointed out that the original attack and all the shooting had come from the Whigs and revealed that the Bank itself had been protected by a force of over two hundred Whig volunteers armed with muskets, some borrowed from the state armory. Bank supporters claimed that the Jacksonians attacked first and criticized the Democratic effort to make the Bank the scapegoat: "The cry of *Bank* ruffians, *Bank* assassins, *Bank* stipendaries, raised whenever an affray happens," one Whig newspaper complained, "is lawless and slanderous in the highest degree." But such a willingness to blame the election violence on the Bank persisted throughout the Democratic party.[57]

Neither side perceived that both were responsible for the violence. The increased emphasis placed upon the masses throughout the Bank War; the demagogic language used to arouse the party faithful; the endless charges and countercharges of fraud, deception, and violence; and the newer, more politically oriented leadership that emerged debased the tone and conduct of politics. Bloodshed became an expected, if not acceptable, part of political life.

An analysis of the 1834 election results shows that the Bank was soundly defeated in the city and across the state. In the combined city-county vote, Democrats went from an average 4,700-vote loss in 1832 to an average 714-vote majority in 1834. Across the state the Congressional delegation shifted from 17 pro-Bank and 11 Democrats elected in 1832 to 11 Whigs and 17 Democrats in 1834. In the state legislature, Democrats won a 41-seat majority, which some feared was so large it might lead to factionalism and infighting. Jacksonians rejoiced that "the most tyrannical faction that has ever ruled a city has received the *coup de grâce* and is expiring under the blows of the people." "The Democratic Party, as it has come out of the struggle of 1834," one Jacksonian exulted in late October, "possesses an overwhelming force, against which no combinations dare appear." Numerous reasons can be given for the Democratic triumph: identification of the Whig party with the Bank, mass hostility to the Bank, revelation of the Bank's role in the panic of 1833–1834, and widespread voter reaction to Whig campaign tactics.[58]

The response of the Democratic party in Philadelphia to the issues and circumstances raised by the Bank War was crucial to the outcome of the struggle. The institution's location and its widespread community support forced city Democrats to be in the vanguard of Jackson's assault on the Bank. They saw the contest as a political struggle and sought to curtail the Bank's political influence. In part, this involved changing the leadership of the Democratic party itself. It also required new tactics, particularly the use of the party masses in town meetings and petition campaigns, and the use of new arguments and issues oriented toward the mass rather than the traditionally active groups.

After an initial period of timidity and restructuring in July of 1832, Philadelphia Democrats responded directly to the issues raised by President Jackson's veto. Their rhetoric reflected these themes, their use of the party masses further swayed the general public, and their campaign efforts, although unsuccessful in Philadelphia, contributed to Democratic victories on the state and national levels.

While most Democrats turned from the Bank to other issues after Jackson's reelection, party members in Philadelphia continued to fight the "monster monopoly." The government directors privately gathered evidence against the Bank for the administration. Party newspapers created a political climate favorable to the removal of the deposits and to Democratic candidates in the elections of 1833 and 1834. Party leaders perfected the tools of mass politics—the town meeting and the petition. They used these tools to publicize the emerging majority sentiment against the Bank, to promote the "bandwagon" effect, and to reinforce the Jacksonian commitment for the separation of the government from the Bank.

After surveying the results of the election of 1834 with its bloodshed and death, both sides recognized that the Bank was a dead issue. Whigs tried to dissociate their party from that issue and to stress others, while Democrats in Philadelphia, confident of their majority status in the city and county and on the state level, resumed intraparty fighting. Unfortunately, this split the party so badly that neither faction's gubernatorial candidate was victorious in 1835. The new ruling Whig-Antimasonic coalition awarded the Bank a state charter as part of the price of victory. In 1836 that state charter became the focus of a reunited Democratic attack, which restored their control over state government until 1848. Throughout the intervening years, Democrats repeatedly returned to the issues and methods perfected during the Bank War to both win elections and avoid more pertinent issues.

NOTES

I wish to acknowledge the financial assistance given this project by the Organized Research Fund of The University of Texas at Arlington.

1. The best illustrations of the various interpretations are Arthur M. Schlesinger, Jr., *The Age of Jackson*; Ralph C. H. Catterall, *The Second Bank of the United States*; Bray Hammond, *Banks and Politics in America: From the Revolution to the Civil War*; Thomas Govan, *Nicholas Biddle: Nationalist and Public Banker, 1786–1844*; Samuel R. Gammon, *The Presidential Campaign of 1832*; James Parton, *The Life of Andrew Jackson*; John S. Bassett, *The Life of Andrew Jackson*; Carl B. Swisher, *Roger B. Taney*; Richard P. McCormick, *The Second American Party System: Party Formation in the Jacksonian Era*; and Robert V. Remini, *Andrew Jackson and the Bank War*.

2. The most prominent of the old leaders were George M. Dallas, Joel B. Sutherland, Charles J. Ingersoll, Henry D. Gilpin, Henry Horn, Thomas Sergeant, and Peter Hay. The rising patronage leaders included James Page, John Pemberton, James N. Barker, Benjamin Mifflin, and John K. Kane.

3. Henry Welsh to Benjamin Bonsall, July 7, 1832, Bonsall Correspondence in the Simon Gratz Collection, Historical Society of Pennsylvania (HSP); Dr. William Jones to John Pemberton, October 1, 1832, ——— Goodwin to Pemberton, October 2, 1832, Pemberton to Jones, October 5, 1832, John Pemberton Papers, HSP; Henry D. Gilpin to Joshua Gilpin, October 6, 1832, Henry D. Gilpin Papers, HSP.

4. Andrew Jackson to Martin Van Buren, December 6, 1831, in John S. Bassett (ed.), *The Correspondence of Andrew Jackson*, IV, 379. The letter relates Jackson's attitudes toward Secretary of the Treasury Louis McLane's report to Congress advocating recharter.

5. *American Sentinel*, March 15, 1831. This view appears in an unsigned article written by Henry D. Gilpin. Gilpin did the piece after dinner with, and at the urging of, Nicholas Biddle. It accurately reflected the majority Democratic sentiment in Philadelphia.

6. For more complete studies of the recharter effort see Bruce I. Ambacher, "George M. Dallas and the Bank War," forthcoming in *Pennsylvania History*, April 1975; Remini, *Jackson and the Bank War*, pp. 73–81; Hammond, *Banks and Politics*, pp. 382–404; Govan, *Biddle*, pp. 169–204; Catterall, *Second Bank*, pp. 164–284. Both former Congressman Charles J. Ingersoll and Congressman Henry Horn, who was also president of "Old Hickory Club #1" in Philadelphia, sought unsuccessfully to obtain a compromise recharter bill from the administration.

7. James D. Richardson (ed.), *A Compilation of the Messages and Papers of the Presidents, 1789–1897*, II, 576–591.

8. George M. Dallas to Gilpin, May 24, July 10, 1832, Dallas to Sophia Dallas (wife), July 9, 11, 1832, George M. Dallas Papers, HSP; William D. Lewis to John D. Lewis, May 6, June 16, July 18, 1832, William D. Lewis to W. Whitney, June 15, 1832, William D. Lewis to R. M. Whitney, June 28, 1832, Lewis-Neilson Papers, HSP; James N. Barker to Pemberton, July 8, 13, 1832, Pemberton Papers; *American Sentinel*, July 2, 1832; *United States Gazette*, July 7, 1832; *Pennsylvanian*, July 9, 1832.

9. *Pennsylvania Inquirer*, July 12, 1832; *Pennsylvanian*, July 13, 1832.

10. *United States Gazette*, July 13, 14, 1832; *National Gazette*, July 14, 1832.

11. Defecting Jacksonians who presided at the rally included Daniel Groves, Charles J. Jack, James Harper, Nathan Jones, John Maitland, and Josiah Randall. *Pennsylvania Inquirer*, July 16, 1832; *United States Gazette*, July 16, 17, 1832; Meyer Moses to Pemberton, July 18, 1832, Pemberton to Moses, July 19, 1832, Pemberton Papers .

12. The officeholders included Senator Dallas, Congressmen Horn and Sutherland, Federal District Attorney Gilpin, Postmaster Page, and District Judge Edward King. Senator Dallas's expression of his own course is illustrative of the expediency felt by many Democrats: "As to the Bank—let that go. We ought to have it, but we can do without it. The attempt to excite hostility to the administration . . . will recoil" (Dallas to Gilpin, July 13, 1832, Gilpin Papers). Pemberton to Moses, July 19, 1832, Pemberton Papers; *American Sentinel*, July 21, 1832; *United States Gazette*, July 23, 1832; *Pennsylvanian*, July 21, 23, 1832; *Pennsylvania Inquirer*, July 23, 1832.

13. Dallas to Bedford Brown, August 1, 1832, in *Trinity College* (N.C.) *Historical Papers*, VI, 68, as quoted in Bassett, *Life of Andrew Jackson*, p. 621; Pemberton to Barnabas Bates, July 24, 1832, Pemberton Papers; George Plitt to James Buchanan, August 1, 1832, James Buchanan Papers, HSP; Henry Horn to James K. Polk, August 7, 1832, in Herbert Weaver (ed.), *The Correspondence of James K. Polk*, I, 490–493; *American Sentinel*, July 24, 1832.

14. *National Gazette*, July 26, 1832.

15. Pennsylvania Democratic dislike of Van Buren was so strong that the delegates ran William Wilkins, the United States senator from Pittsburgh, as a favorite-son vice-presidential candidate and voted the state's thirty electoral votes for Jackson and Wilkins (*National Gazette*, July 14, 26, August 2, September 20, October 4, 1832; *United States Gazette*, July 13, 16, 23, 25, 26, 31, August 8, 28, September 12,

19, October 3, 4, 1832; *Pennsylvania Inquirer,* July 13, 19, 21, 24, August 8, 28, September 28, 1832).

16. Barker to Pemberton, July 8, 13, 1832, Pemberton to Moses, July 19, 1832, Pemberton Papers; *Pennsylvanian,* July 9, 12, 23, 25, 30, August 20, September 1, 3, 7, 10, 17, 20, 26, October 1, 1832; *American Sentinel,* July 16, 21, 23, 24, 30, September 29, October 1, 1832.

17. *Pennsylvanian,* September 10, October 5, 6, 9, 1832; *American Sentinel,* September 22, 1832; *United States Gazette,* September 19, October 3, 5, 1832; *National Gazette,* October 4, 1832; *Pennsylvania Inquirer,* September 28, 1832.

18. *United States Gazette,* October 11, 1832; Joseph Sill Diary, October 8, 9, 1832, HSP.

Candidate	District	Party	Vote
Gowan, James	1	Nat. Rep.	1,916
*Sutherland, Joel B.	1	Democrat	2,366
Davis, Samuel R.	1	Ultra Veto Dem.	451
Binney, Horace	2	Nat. Rep.	5,364
*Harper, James	2	Nat. Rep.	5,104
Richards, Benjamin	2	Democrat	3,396
*Horn, Henry	2	Democrat	3,194
*Watmough, John G.	3	Nat. Rep.	4,041
Burden, Jessie R.	3	Democrat	2,268

(Incumbents starred)

The results are not quite as pro-Bank as they seem since the attitude of Joel B. Sutherland and John G. Watmough toward the Bank was not entirely clear. Watmough later became a sycophant of the Bank and Sutherland became an opponent.

19. Wolf privately complained that the people had "of their own accord without consulting" him coupled him with Jackson. He believed that had been responsible for his significant loss of votes and complained he had never been afforded the opportunity of showing how unjust that connection was. Yet he had never publicly committed himself either way and apparently rode the Jacksonian bandwagon and then complained when he got caught in the Bank furor. See Wolf to Roberts Vaux, October 18, 1832, George Wolf Papers, HSP.

20. *United States Gazette,* October 11, 1832.

21. Ibid., October 17, 18, 20, November 1, 1832; *National Gazette,* October 20, 25, November 1, 2, 1832; Gammon, *Campaign of 1832,* p. 154.

22. Gilpin to Joshua Gilpin, October 13, 1832, Gilpin to Louis Mc-

Lane, October 19, 1832, Gilpin Papers; Pemberton to John Pemberton, October 14, 1932, Pemberton Papers; William J. Duane to Isaac D. Barnard, October 22, 1832, Townsend-LeMaistre Collection, HSP; *Pennsylvanian*, October 10, 16, 19, 29, 30, November 1, 2, 1832; *American Sentinel*, October 19, 20, 26, 31, November 2, 1832.

23. Gilpin to Edward Livingston, November 3, 1832, Gilpin Papers; Pemberton to Jackson, November 5, 1832, Pemberton Papers; *American Sentinel*, November 2, 1832; *National Gazette*, November 15, 1832.

24. The statement was made by John Brown in Pemberton to Jackson, December 15, 1832, Pemberton Papers; Pemberton to McLane, December 8, 1832, Barker to Pemberton, December 10, 1832, ibid.; Dallas to Sophia Dallas (wife), December 1, 1832, Dallas Papers.

25. The government directors for 1833 were Hugh McElderry of Baltimore, Saul Alley of New York, and John T. Sullivan, Henry D. Gilpin, and Peter Wager of Philadelphia. The commissions, signed by Jackson and Livingston, January 3, 1833, are in the Etting, Bank of the United States Collection, HSP, IV, 86; Gilpin to Dallas, January 5, 1833, Gilpin to John K. Kane, January 5, 1833, Gilpin to McLane, January 7, 1833, Gilpin Papers; Govan, *Biddle*, p. 224. Senator Dallas, for example, labeled Wager "a fat, foolish and unpopular man, . . . a bag of wind . . . and a cup of limed hemlock" (Dallas to Gilpin, January 10, 1833, Gilpin Papers).

26. Gilpin to Dallas, January 12, 1833, Gilpin to Senator Josiah S. Johnston, January 14, 1833, Gilpin Papers; John L. Hodge to Johnston, January 10, 1833, Josiah S. Johnston Papers, HSP; Govan, *Biddle*, p. 225. The plan to cast blank votes in the presidential election was devised by Dallas and Gilpin. Late in January, Gilpin assessed the board meetings as follows: "It is a misuse of the terms *directed*. They know absolutely nothing. There is no consultation, no exchanges of sentiments, no production of correspondence, but merely a rapid, superficial, general statement or a reference to a committee which will probably never report" (Gilpin to Dallas, January 26, 1833, Gilpin Papers).

27. Gilpin, Bank of the United States Diary, March 5, 6, 9, 1833, Gilpin Papers; "Questions as to a Bank of the United States," March 19, 1833, in Bassett (ed.), *Correspondence of Jackson*, V, 32–33; Govan, *Biddle*, pp. 227–229.

28. Gilpin, Bank of the United States Diary, April 6, 8, 9, 17, 21, 22, 23, 1833, Gilpin Papers; Jackson to J. Sullivan, P. Wager, and H. D. Gilpin, April 14, 1833, in Bassett (ed.), *Correspondence of Jackson*, V, 59; *Pennsylvanian*, April 9, 1833; Gilpin to Livingston, April 11, 1833, Gilpin Papers; Govan, *Biddle*, pp. 229–231. Jackson's letter to the government directors was drafted by Amos Kendall.

29. P. M. Fox to Pemberton, November 20, 1832, Pemberton Papers; Richardson (ed.), *Messages of the Presidents*, II, 599–600; *Pennsylvanian*, March 21, 23, April 1, 1833. The arguments for removal included past Bank deception and delay in payment of the public debt, overextension of loans, falsified statements to the secretary of the treasury, exclusion of the government directors from decisions, and inability to return the deposits.

30. George M. Dallas, "Greetings in Behalf of the Young Men of the City and County of Philadelphia," June 8, 1833, Dallas Papers; *Pennsylvanian*, June 5, 7, 8, 10, 1833; *American Sentinel*, June 10, 1833; *United States Gazette*, June 10, 1833; J. Thomas Scharf and Thompson Westcott, *History of Philadelphia, 1609–1884*, I, 636–637.

31. S. Bushearn & John L. Woolf to Dallas, June 17, 1833, Dallas to Bushearn & Woolf, June 18, 1833, Dallas Papers; *Pennsylvanian*, June 7, 12, 13, 14, 19, 23, July 1, 4, 5, 8, 9, 10, 11, 15, 31, 1833; *American Sentinel*, June 18, 19, 1833. The *Pennsylvanian* criticized Page's meeting as "disunity bent."

32. *American Sentinel*, July 26, 1833; *Pennsylvanian*, July 16, 20, 26, 27, 29, 31, August 1, 1833.

33. *Pennsylvanian*, August 6, 7, 8, 9, 10, 1833; *American Sentinel*, August 6, 7, 8, 9, 21, 1833.

34. Jackson to Sullivan, Gilpin, and Wager, August 3, 1833, Sullivan and Wager to Gilpin, August 7, 1833, Gilpin, Bank of the United States Diary, August 12, 13, 15, 16, 19, 1833, Gilpin Papers; Kendall to Jackson, August 25, 1833, in Bassett (ed.), *Correspondence of Jackson*, V, 169–170; Jackson to Polk, August 31, 1833, in Weaver (ed.), *Correspondence of Polk*, II, 106.

35. Gilpin to Kendall, September 7, 1833, Gilpin Papers; *American Sentinel*, September 6, 1833; *Pennsylvanian*, September 9, 14, 18, 21, 24, 25, 1833.

36. *Pennsylvania Inquirer*, September 21, 23, 24, 28, 1833; *National Gazette*, September 24, 26, 28, 1833; *United States Gazette*, September 23, 27, 28, 1833.

37. *Pennsylvanian*, October 2, 1833; *United States Gazette*, October 3, 1833.

38. *American Sentinel*, October 4, 1833.

39. Ibid., October 8, 1833; *Pennsylvanian*, October 8, 1833.

40. *American Sentinel*, October 11, 19, 22, 1833. Sutherland had resigned his congressional seat at the end of the session in March 1833. Governor Wolf then appointed him as a judge in Philadelphia. In September, Sutherland resigned that judgeship to run for his old House seat. John Sergeant's connections to the Bank, as counsel and director, and to

the National Republican party, as its 1832 vice-presidential candidate, made the election a referendum on the Bank and removal. Sutherland beat Sergeant 2,835 to 2,139.

41. Gilpin supplied Senators Thomas Hart Benton, John Forsyth, and William Wilkins with technical data they used in speeches against the Bank. See Gilpin to Kane, December 19, 1833, Gilpin to Roger B. Taney, December 19, 1833, Gilpin to John Forsyth, December 22, 1833, Gilpin to Thomas Hart Benton, December 22, 26, 1833, Gilpin to William Wilkins, December 28, 1833, Gilpin Papers; *Congressional Register of Debates*, 23rd Cong., 1st Sess., p. 375; *National Gazette*, December 13, 1833; *United States Gazette*, December 19, 20, 28, 1833; *Pennsylvania Inquirer*, December 16, 17, 18, 28, 1833; *Pennsylvanian*, December 30, 1833; *American Sentinel*, December 17, 20, 31, 1833.

42. *National Gazette*, January 2, 1834; *Pennsylvanian*, January 2, 3, 1834; *American Sentinel*, January 2, 3, 1834.

43. *National Gazette*, January 2, 1834; *Pennsylvanian*, January 4, 1834.

44. Nicholas Biddle to Joseph Hopkinson, February 21, 1834, Joseph Hopkinson Papers, HSP; *American Sentinel*, January 13, February 27, 1834; *United States Gazette*, February 3, 24, 1834; *National Gazette*, February 13, 22, 25, 1834; *Pennsylvanian*, January 8, February 26, 1834; Marquis James, *Andrew Jackson: Portrait of a President*, p. 365.

45. The resolutions and toasts called the Bank such things as "the great juggernaut of the aristocracy," "a Vampyre . . . attempting to sustain itself by the destruction of others," "a mutinous soldier," and "the *servant*, it aspires to be the *master* of the people . . . in its downfall the republic will crush a *serpent* that would sting it" (resolutions of the Southwark Meeting of January 22, 1834, by Dallas and Gilpin in Gilpin, Bank of the United States Diary, Gilpin Papers; Dallas to Wolf, January 23, 1834, Vaux to Wolf, February 13, 1834, Wolf Papers; A. J. Pleasanton to Buchanan, January 20, 1834, Buchanan Papers; Henry Horn to Polk, January 31, 1834, in Weaver [ed.], *Correspondence of Polk*, II, 284–285; Pemberton to Jackson, January 31, February 6, 1834, Pemberton Papers; *National Gazette*, January 27, February 13, 1834; *American Sentinel*, January 30, 31, February 10, 27, 1834; *Pennsylvanian*, January 28, February 6, 1834).

46. Wolf to Vaux, January 23, 1834, Dallas to Wolf, February 26, March 2, 1834, Wolf Papers; *National Gazette*, January 29, 30, March 1, 1834; *United States Gazette*, January 20, 22, 23, 25, February 28, March 1, 3, 1834; *Pennsylvanian*, January 20, 24, February 27, March 1, 8, 1834; *Pennsylvania Inquirer*, March 1, 1834; Charles M. Snyder, *The Jacksonian Heritage: Pennsylvania Politics, 1833–1848*, pp. 39–41.

47. Dallas to Wolf, February 27, March 2, 4, 1834, Vaux to Wolf,

March 4, 1834, Wolf to Vaux, March 6, 1834, Wolf Papers; *American Sentinel*, March 4, 5, 1834; *Pennsylvanian*, March 3, 4, 5, 1834; *United States Gazette*, March 5, 7, 1834; *National Gazette*, March 4, 1834; *Pennsylvania Inquirer*, February 28, March 1, 1834; William M. Meigs, *The Life of Charles Jared Ingersoll*, p. 183.

48. *Pennsylvania Inquirer*, April 22, 23, 1834; *United States Gazette*, April 22, 23, 1834; *Pennsylvanian*, April 22, 23, 1834; *American Sentinel*, April 22, 23, 1834.

49. Dallas to Wolf, April 24, 1834, Wolf Papers; *Pennsylvanian*, May 9, 12, 14, 1834; *American Sentinel*, May 12, June 25, 1834; *Pennsylvania Inquirer*, May 13, June 6, 1834; *National Gazette*, May 29, 1834.

50. Vaux to Wolf, July 19, 1834, Wolf Papers; *National Gazette*, July 26, 1834; *Pennsylvanian*, July 16, 1834; *American Sentinel*, July 17, 1834.

51. In his correspondence with Governor Wolf, Attorney General Dallas frequently noted this steady decline in Bank support. He found Bank supporters evolving from an agitated state to one he described as "gross, foul, and intemperate" as they realized "the game . . . is nearly played out, and . . . the democratic party . . . will ultimately prove victorious." Prior to the campaigning in 1834 he reported "an irresistible spirit seems to be spreading, hostile to the Bank and in favor of the general government" (Dallas to Wolf, March 24, April 24, August 17, 1834, Wolf Papers).

52. The guests of the day included Senators Thomas Hart Benton, Isaac Hill, Felix Grundy, and John Tipton and Congressmen William Allen, Robert Lytle, and George Gilmer. Their presence confirms that anti-Bank sentiment was growing (Gilpin to Van Buren, July 4, 1834, Martin Van Buren Papers, Library of Congress [LC]; Dallas to Wolf, July 9, 1834, Wolf Papers; *Pennsylvanian*, May 5, 6, 7, 9, July 4, 7, 8, 9, 12, 15, 17, 1834; *American Sentinel*, June 9, July 4, 8, 10, 1834).

53. Dallas to Wolf, August 17, 29, September 4, 21, October 26, 31, 1834, Wolf Papers; Gilpin to Van Buren, August 31, 1834, Van Buren Papers; *American Sentinel*, September 11, 18, 22, 1834; *Pennsylvanian*, September 17, 19, 1834; Snyder, *Jacksonian Heritage*, p. 49.

54. *American Sentinel*, September 24, 1834; *Pennsylvanian*, September 29, 1834.

55. *Pennsylvanian*, September 29, 1834; *American Sentinel*, September 29, 1834.

56. *Pennsylvanian*, October 3, 4, 1834; *National Gazette*, October 6, 14, 1834; Scharf and Westcott, *History of Philadelphia*, I, 638.

57. *American Sentinel*, October 16, 1834; *Pennsylvanian*, October 27, 1834; *Pennsylvania Inquirer*, November 18, 1834; *National Gazette*, October 16, 17, December 6, 1834; Scharf and Westcott, *History of*

Philadelphia, I, 638–639. President Jackson blamed the election violence on the Whigs in his Annual Message of December 1834 (Richardson [ed.], *Messages of the Presidents*, III, 108–112).

58. Dallas to Wolf, October 26, 31, 1834, Vaux to Wolf, November 2, 1834, Wolf Papers; Andrew Beaumont to Polk, October 17, 1834, in Weaver (ed.), *Correspondence of Polk*, II, 532; *Pennsylvanian*, October 15, 17, 21, 22, 23, November 3, 1834; *American Sentinel*, October 20, 21, November 4, 7, 21, 1834; Henry R. Mueller, *The Whig Party in Pennsylvania*, p. 18; Snyder, *Jacksonian Heritage*, pp. 48–49.

Candidate	District	Party	Vote
*Sutherland, Joel B.	1	Democrat	3,782
Gowan, James	1	Whig	2,345
*Harper, James	2	Whig	5,560
Ingersoll, Joseph R.	2	Whig	5,589
Linnard, James L.	2	Democrat	3,710
Horn, Henry	2	Democrat	3,671
*Watmough, John G.	3	Whig	4,598
Ash, Michael	3	Democrat	5,757

(Incumbents starred)

BIBLIOGRAPHY

Manuscript Material

American Philosophical Society, Philadelphia
    John K. Kane Papers
Historical Society of Pennsylvania, Philadelphia
    James Buchanan Papers
    George M. Dallas Papers
    Frank M. Etting, Bank of the United States Collection
    Henry D. Gilpin Papers
    Simon Gratz Collection
    Joseph Hopkinson Papers
    Josiah S. Johnston Papers
    Lewis-Neilson Papers
    John Pemberton Papers
    Townsend-LeMaistre Collection
    Roberts Vaux Papers
    George Wolf Papers
Library of Congress, Washington, D.C.
    Nicholas Biddle Papers
    Andrew Jackson Papers
    Martin Van Buren Papers
University of Pennsylvania Library, Philadelphia
    William Porter, Bank of the United States Collection

Published Material

Ambacher, Bruce I. "George M. Dallas and the Bank War," forthcoming in *Pennsylvania History*, April 1975.

American Sentinel, Philadelphia.

Bartlett, Margueritte G. *The Chief Phases of Pennsylvania Politics in the Jacksonian Period*. Allentown, Pa.: H. R. Haas and Company, 1919.

Bassett, John S. *The Life of Andrew Jackson*. New York: Macmillan Co., 1928.

_____, ed. *The Correspondence of Andrew Jackson*. 6 vols. Washington, D.C.: Carnegie Institution, 1926–1935.

Catterall, Ralph C. H. *The Second Bank of the United States*. Chicago: University of Chicago Press, 1902.

Fitzpatrick, John, ed. *The Autobiography of Martin Van Buren*. Washington, D.C.: American Historical Association Annual Report, 1918.

Gammon, Samuel R. *The Presidential Campaign of 1832*. Baltimore: Johns Hopkins Press, 1922.

Govan, Thomas. *Nicholas Biddle: Nationalist and Public Banker, 1786–1844*. Chicago: University of Chicago Press, 1959.

Hammond, Bray. *Banks and Politics in America: From the Revolution to the Civil War*. Princeton: Princeton University Press, 1957.

James, Marquis. *Andrew Jackson: Portrait of a President*. New York: Bobbs-Merrill, 1937.

Klein, Philip S. *Pennsylvania Politics, 1817–1832: A Game without Rules*. Philadelphia: Historical Society of Pennsylvania, 1940.

McCormick, Richard P. *The Second American Party System: Party Formation in the Jacksonian Era*. Chapel Hill: University of North Carolina Press, 1966.

Meigs, William M. *The Life of Charles Jared Ingersoll*. Philadelphia: J. B. Lippincott Co., 1897.

Mueller, Henry R. *The Whig Party in Pennsylvania*. New York: Columbia University Press, 1922.

National Gazette, Philadelphia.

Parton, James. *The Life of Andrew Jackson*. New York: Harper and Row, 1861.

Pennsylvania Inquirer, Philadelphia.

Pennsylvanian, Philadelphia.

Remini, Robert V. *Andrew Jackson and the Bank War*. New York: W. W. Norton Co., 1967.

Richardson, James D., ed. *A Compilation of the Messages and Papers of the Presidents, 1789–1897*. 10 vols. Washington, D.C., 1907.

Scharf, J. Thomas, and Thompson Westcott. *History of Philadelphia, 1609–1884*. 3 vols. Philadelphia: L. H. Everts and Co., 1884.

Schlesinger, Arthur M., Jr. *The Age of Jackson*. Boston: Little, Brown and Co., 1946.

Snyder, Charles M. *The Jacksonian Heritage: Pennsylvania Politics, 1833–1848*. Harrisburg, Pa.: Pennsylvania Historical and Museum Commission, 1958.

Swisher, Carl B. *Roger B. Taney*. New York: Macmillan Co., 1935.

United States Gazette, Philadelphia.

Washington Globe, Washington, D.C.

Weaver, Herbert, ed. *The Correspondence of James K. Polk*. 2 vols. Nashville: Vanderbilt University, 1969.

Fort Worth and the Progressive Era: The Movement for Charter Revision, 1899–1907

BY RICHARD G. MILLER

THE MOST ENDURING REFORMS secured during the Progressive Era were those designed to remodel municipal government. Such reforms as municipal ownership of utilities, regulated rates for urban transportation, initiative, referendum, nonpartisan ballot, and commission and city-manager forms of government changed the governmental structure of urban America. City dwellers supported reforms because they were convinced that city government needed these changes to make it efficient and free from machine rule.[1]

Of all the adjustments made in municipal affairs the commission and city-manager plans have achieved the greatest impact.[2] Recent historical analysis of this reform has centered chiefly on the motives of reformers in bringing about this overhaul in the municipal structure. Professors James Weinstein and Samuel Hays have warned that no adequate understanding as to why the commission and city-manager plans were adopted can be attempted without explaining the political forces behind the changes.[3] They have contended that the business community sponsored and led the efforts to secure this reform. Businessmen of the era, they argue, had a two-fold purpose in advocating the commission and city-manager plans: to rationalize city government and make it more efficient and responsive to the needs of an industrial community, and to win control of municipal affairs from the local political bosses.[4]

To test this thesis, the circumstances of how and why one city adopted commission government need to be examined. In this way the efforts to secure reform can be analyzed to determine what forces led a community like Fort Worth, Texas, to alter dramatically its municipal structure from a ward system of representation to one that elected the city council at large and reduced its size. Moreover, the question of how commission government affected the way people perceived their city government should be answered. Did commission government bring about more democracy as its supporters claimed or did it merely destroy ward representation and participation in city affairs?

Fort Worth, which approved commission government in 1907, seems an ideal city in which to determine if the business community did indeed lead the efforts to secure that form of municipal government. That city's dramatic population growth and industrial expansion during the Progressive Era resulted directly from the aggressiveness of its business leaders. Fort Worth businessmen had made the city the merchandising center for West Texas cattlemen and farmers.[5] In addition, in 1901 they attracted the packing-house industry, which achieved remarkable growth and in turn attracted other manufacturing enterprises.[6] At the beginning of the twentieth century, Fort Worth's population stood at 26,688. By 1920 it had reached 106,482. The demographic complexion of Fort Worth differed sharply from many other expanding industrial communities because the vast majority of its population migrated from southern and border states, not from foreign countries.[7] In fact, Fort

Worth had a foreign-born population of only 6.7 percent in 1900 and 5.7 percent in 1910. The city's black population was 15.9 percent and 18.1 percent for the same years.[8] In religious affiliation, Fort Worth's population belonged chiefly to the Baptist, Methodist, and Presbyterian churches, thus giving the community an evangelical Protestant tone.[9]

The campaign for commission government began in 1899. At first reformers sought to revise Fort Worth's charter to include changes that many thought necessary to meet the needs of a growing city. By 1899 some Fort Worth businessmen recognized that the rapid growth in population and industry brought with it increased demands for city services. The populace needed an increased water supply, street improvements, better police protection, and efficient budgetary and accounting procedures.[10] In 1899 a few businessmen proposed to the Texas legislature that changes be made in the city's charter to give Fort Worth a tax plan providing sufficient revenue to meet the city's needs for streets, schools, and water. In addition, city government would be given control of its courts and power to enforce health regulations and to establish salaries for its public officials.

But when these reforms emerged from the legislature, Mayor Buckley B. Paddock and many other community leaders opposed them on the grounds that they did not go far enough.[11] Alderman Thomas Powell objected to the revisions because they did not give the city the power to regulate and tax franchises issued by the city council.[12] Powell, in fact, became the spokesman for Fort Worth businessmen who organized the Board of Trade. Control of city government, they believed, should not rest in the hands of local politicians who might come under control of special interests.[13] Powell and others feared that the city council, a body composed of one alderman from each of the city's nine wards, would come under the domination of the growing number of utility and street railway companies seeking franchises

in Fort Worth.[14] They saw a need to professionalize city government to improve its ability to regulate private capitalism for
the good of the entire city. In fact, this first effort to revise the
city's charter united the business community to seek more far-
reaching alterations in Fort Worth's charter.

The goals envisioned by the city-oriented businessmen brought
them into sharp conflict with the existing political system. The
city council served as the vehicle through which each ward had
a voice in city affairs. By this method of government, men
elected as aldermen tended to place the interests of their ward
above any long-range plans sought by the business community.
Of the sixteen aldermen who served between 1900 and 1907,
ten were small businessmen or managerial types who had strong
economic ties to their neighborhoods. For example, William
Ward, who represented the First Ward, owned the White Ele-
phant Saloon, and Jack Lehane, from the Fourth Ward, was a
railroad freight agent. The remainder were four attorneys and
two businessmen. Among the attorneys, only one, Eugene Orrick, supported reform measures throughout his terms. The
others were professional politicians. The two businessmen, William Newby, a bank president, and Edward Maddox, owner of
a large ice manufacturing company, backed reform because they
did business on a city-wide scale and wanted a government more
responsive to their needs.[15]

The city election of 1900 reflected this growing concern
among Fort Worth businessmen. Since Fort Worth was essentially a one-party city, the Democratic primary served as the chief
election.[16] In December 1899, Thomas Powell announced his
intention to oppose incumbent Mayor Buckley B. Paddock, who
had held the post since 1892. Powell and Paddock both had
similar backgrounds: each had migrated to Fort Worth to make
his fortune and both were former newspapermen and practicing

attorneys. Powell had been city attorney and in 1899 had been elected an alderman to fill an unexpired term.[17]

Powell made reform the central theme of his campaign. He declared that the source of "all municipal government lies in the people, and that municipal governments are formed for the public good and not for private gain." He expressed the concerns of many businessmen and professionals when he opposed the development of "municipal rings" and "machines." Powell believed that city government could not respond to the needs of an industrialized community if it were controlled by local politicians who might come under the influence of special interests. Like other so-called reformers, he wanted to use the rhetoric of democracy to defeat men opposed to him. Throughout the campaign Powell hammered that "there should be no partisan politics in the mayor's office," and that machine politics "are always organized, controlled, and perpetuated for private plunder." They deny, he argued, the "people a government in their interest." He thought that the mayor's post was a full-time job and should be run in a "business fashion." He favored civil service for municipal employees, a separate and elected school board, a referendum upon "all matters which impose burdens upon the tax payers," an improved water system that would meet the present and future needs of the city, and street improvements that would cut down on the "dust problem." In short, Powell favored running city government "as a businessman runs his own business."[18] Fort Worth businessmen wanted to control city government but to do so in the name of the people. In the reformer's mind their own economic prosperity and that of "the people" were one and the same. To such men as Powell, reform meant that control of Fort Worth should reside within the business community.[19] The faith that reformers placed in business methods and their desire to apply them to

government reflected the achievements of the industrial revolution. In the minds of upper- and middle-class reformers, business technology had vastly improved the quality of life. If it had
succeeded in the private sector, why not apply it to government?

Paddock based his campaign on his record. He proposed no
reforms and in fact hardly exerted himself during the contest.[20]
Consequently, when the Democratic primary results came in,
Paddock found his bid for a fifth term thwarted. In fact, the
voters not only chose Powell over Paddock but they also ousted
all the incumbent aldermen, save one, from office.[21] This clean
sweep indicated that voters had been sold on Powell through
his reform rhetoric and in the process had given him a new city
council to put into practice the measures he advocated.

Powell did not wait long in taking action. Two weeks after
he assumed office, Powell delivered to the city council his proposals for remodeling city government. He wanted a new city
charter that would limit the powers of the city council by giving
the voters the right to elect the various department heads, such
as city attorney and fire chief. He also demanded that the new
charter should not permit the city council to grant franchises
for public utilities unless a sufficient compensation was paid
based on the gross receipts of the franchise holder. Finally, he
included a proposal for the initiative and referendum.[22] These
reforms had the support of the city's business leaders, who
wanted to see city government run on a more "efficient basis."
The intent of these changes seems obvious. In advocating at-
large elections, reformers could more easily dilute the voting
power of lower-class voters. Moreover, the particularistic interests of each ward would lose their significance in city-wide
elections. By removing the appointment power of the city council and giving it to the "people," candidates would be controlled
more easily by business leaders, since they would be running in
city-wide races.

To arouse support for a new charter, Powell suggested that a committee be appointed from many of the city's interest groups. This proposed charter committee would have representatives from the Board of Trade, lawyers, bankers, city council, and labor.[23] Businessmen would dominate such a group, and the interests of the people would in reality mean the interests of business. Powell and the Board of Trade succeeded in winning popular endorsement for the new charter from labor and the newspapers.[24] In addition to the election of city officials, initiative, and referendum, Powell sought an eight-hour day for city employees and all city repair work done by "laboring men of Fort Worth."[25] Even in this proposal the designs of the business community seemed clear. By supporting city workers, they won labor's backing for their other proposals, thus strengthening their own designs for controlling city government. Labor organizations, such as the Trades Assembly and Building Trades Council, sponsored meetings and even held a city-wide rally to drum up support for a new charter. At the mass meeting, union men passed a resolution calling for election by the people of the mayor, aldermen, board of equalization, school board, chief of police, tax assessor and collector, superintendent of waterworks, fire chief, auditor, city secretary, city attorney, city physician, city engineer, city treasurer, and street commissioner. They also endorsed the eight-hour day and voter approval for all franchises. One union official sarcastically asked, ". . . is it possible for nine men or a majority of nine men to better judge the qualifications of the men who carry on the business of the city than . . . the thousands of intelligent citizens of this city?—do not believe it."[26]

In spite of this outpouring of support, the city council passed its own charter revision plan. The council wanted to continue to elect most of the department heads, with the exception of the chief of police, tax assessor and collector, and the board of equalization. The aldermen opposed inclusion of the initiative, referendum, and eight-hour day in the charter.[27] After the council passed its charter revision, it adopted a plan that called for submission of it to a convention composed of three members from the city council, three from the Board of Trade, three from labor organizations, and three elected members from each of the nine wards.[28] This plan would allow the ward politicians to control the convention through their political connections in their respective wards.

Mayor Powell and his supporters from the Board of Trade, labor, and the newspapers rejected the council's plan. In fact, Powell vetoed the ordinance calling for the convention. The *Fort Worth Morning Register* accused the aldermen of not keeping faith with the people. The paper contended that all changes in the charter had been discussed in detail at the last election and that Powell had been elected on that platform. "The new aldermen have used the present charter as a model and followed it in retaining in the hands of the council the control of city government," the editor wrote. "They propose to boss this town." Powell proclaimed that the people's competence to elect their own officials "cannot be changed by all the councils in the country." He added that "whenever you strip the citizen of the right of self-government you strike a blow at civil liberty and the rights of the people."[29] This loggerhead between reformers and the city council represented the power struggle going on in Fort Worth. To the aldermen, control over city patronage represented the basis of their political power. If the council could not name department heads, it lost the ability to influence those persons to appoint their constituents to city jobs. Moreover, if the council lost control of franchises, aldermen no longer could bring pressure on utilities and street railways to increase services in their respective wards. A potential source of revenue for aldermen and ward politicians also might be lost.[30]

Indeed, it was precisely this system that many businessmen and professionals opposed. They wanted a city government that could respond to the increasing needs of an industrial community without having to make arrangements with local politicians. They believed that, if control over city departments and the granting of franchises were turned over to the people at large, the men elected and the franchises granted would be controlled from the meeting rooms of the Board of Trade. Fort Worth's businessmen had grand dreams for their city's growth, but they wanted an efficient city government that would be more responsive to their needs.[31]

A majority of the city council had blocked efforts to strip it of its political power. Aldermen did not seem to fear the outrage in public opinion that the mayor, newspapers, Board of Trade, and labor organizations had predicted. To demonstrate their confidence, they sustained Powell's veto for a charter convention.[32] The *Register*, after the council's action, pointed to the frustration that reformers felt. The paper indicated that the public could only protest and defeat the council's proposed charter, leaving the city with its present one. "In either case, the administration of the city's affairs is to be kept closely in the hands of the city council, which being itself elected by the people holds that the people are incapable of electing the best men to office."[33]

The scene now shifted to the legislature. Fort Worth's representative in the House, John Y. Hogsett, introduced a bill similar to the one demanded by Powell, but the city council sent a delegation to lobby against it. Soon the legislature dropped the whole issue of Fort Worth's charter, since the two factions involved could not reach an agreement. As it appeared that no new charter would emerge, the leaders of the Board of Trade hammered out a compromise that made some improvement over the previous charter. This agreement emerged from a "citizen meeting" sponsored by the Board of Trade, but which was in reality a gathering of the city council and business leaders. The compromise allowed the city to increase the property-tax limit, to improve streets and water, and to pay off the city debt.[34] None of the so-called reforms that Powell wanted were included; instead he and other reformers settled for a charter they did not like with the hope that it was only the beginning.

Powell did not waste any time in renewing his efforts for reform. In his annual message, the mayor challenged the city council: "Shall the people own the city and its government or shall it be owned by selfish interests; shall the city council control and govern the city against the people's will or in accordance with public approval?" He demanded initiative, referendum, civil service for city employees, and city regulation of utilities and street railways.[35] In fact, Powell's message proved the opening salvo in the efforts by reformers to win control of city council. In the Democratic primary campaign, held in December 1901, reformers made every effort to find candidates who would be more acceptable to their views. At the same time, the aldermen and their supporters in the wards controlled the machinery of the Democratic party and set the date of election for December 21, 1901, the last Saturday before Christmas. Local Democratic politicians intended this rather blatant political move to hold down the vote of many businessmen and their clerks who favored the reforms advocated by Powell and the Board of Trade. Moreover, the executive committee allowed only two weeks for the campaign, seriously weakening the prospects of aldermanic candidates seeking to oust incumbents.[36]

In the nine races for aldermen, all but one incumbent stood for reelection. Only two aldermen, Eugene Orrick and William Newby of the Sixth and Eighth wards, respectively, came out for reforming the charter.[37] Both Orrick and Newby represented different interest groups than did the others on the council. Orrick, an attorney, and Newby, a bank president, saw the need to place men in city government who wanted to improve the overall efficiency of municipal affairs. They did not believe Fort Worth could become a major city until control of city hall was wrestled from the hands of local politicians. In the minds of reformers, the particularistic interests of the ward heelers—who had forged alliances with small businessmen, saloon owners, and the lower classes—could not move Fort Worth to meet the challenges brought by increased urbanization and industrialization.[38]

The election results proved another setback for reformers when voters returned all incumbent aldermen. The only close race occurred in the Sixth Ward, where reformer Orrick squeaked to victory by 16 votes out of a total of 260. The voter turnout of 60.5 percent of those registered indicated that in spite of the date of the election a large percentage of the voters made their way to the polls.[39] The election demonstrated that incumbent aldermen could win elections in their respective wards in spite of the efforts of the Board of Trade and the city's labor organizations. The local ward politicians had established effective organizations within their wards by providing city jobs for supporters, doing favors for their constituents at city hall, and looking out for the interests of their wards in city council. None of the six aldermen who opposed charter reform made any secret of their feelings. In fact, they made a virtue of their opposition. The appeal by reformers that Fort Worth needed a more direct city-wide democracy had little effect on the way the voters selected their aldermen. It seemed that the voters could not perceive any direct benefit to their own interests by voting out of office men who had been looking after their welfare at city hall.

Nevertheless, Powell and the Board of Trade renewed their efforts in 1902 and 1903 to develop a new charter for Fort

Worth that would in their minds meet the demands of a growing city. During this period Fort Worth businessmen persuaded
Armour and Swift & Company to establish packing houses in
North Fort Worth.[40] This industry increased the demands for
more city services, such as street improvements, street railways,
and a greater water supply. As more people and industry moved
to Fort Worth, business leaders thought it imperative that they
win control of city government.[41] At the same time the reformers
found a new means by which this effort might succeed—the introduction in Texas of the poll tax.[42] This amendment went into
effect in 1903 and would by all estimates sharply reduce the
number of voters. This tax would strike hardest at the lower
class, which had provided the strongest support to the ward
politicians. One Fort Worth newspaper declared that "among
those who paid their taxes only the better class of colored people was represented and much of the irresponsible white vote
was banned by the tax restrictions." The city poll tax in Fort
Worth was set at $1.00 and for county and state elections $1.75,
which meant that every year a man must produce $2.75 to exer-
cise his franchise.[43] These predictions proved accurate, for, in
the Democratic city primary held in January 1904, the vote was
reduced by almost half of the total three years earlier.[44]

As the election neared, reformers seemed unable to field a
slate of candidates to run against those aldermen opposed to
charter reform. Of the nine races, only five aldermen had any
opposition at all. Reformers began to realize that it was extremely difficult to defeat a local politician who had made an effort
to meet and know most voters in his ward.[45] Even the poll tax
and the all-white primary, a new dimension in Fort Worth elections, could not convince businessmen or other professionals
to run for election within their own wards. Indeed, the election
results indicated that the new city council would be essentially

the same as the previous one in its opposition to a reform charter.[46]

After the 1904 Democratic primary, city elections took an unexpected turn when both the Republican and Socialist parties announced they would field candidates in the general election. This opposition had the effect of uniting Democrats and forcing them to deal with the reforms proposed by Powell and his supporters on the Board of Trade.[47] For the first time since the campaign for charter reform began, Democrats were called upon to defend their record, and by so doing they strengthened the efforts of the business community to bring major changes to city government. The need for paved streets, accurate assessment of real property, street railways that would connect Fort Worth with the growing communities surrounding the city, and improved sewage facilities were all discussed in detail during the campaign.[48] The results of the election demonstrated that, although Fort Worth voters did not consider either Republicans or Socialists a viable alternative to Democrats, they did want city services improved. In the race for mayor, Powell polled 83.7 percent of the vote. The aldermanic results were similar to Powell's margin.[49]

After the 1904 city elections, reformers began an intensive campaign to persuade the city council of the necessity of revising municipal government. They had almost a year before the next session of the legislature to win widespread public support for the reforms they had advocated since 1899. Powell kicked off the campaign in his annual message. He renewed his pleas for franchise regulation, municipal ownership of utilities, improved streets, election of all department heads, initiative, referendum, and civil service for municipal employees, and a referendum on the granting of city franchises. "I am convinced," he declared, "that no public franchise should be given away or sold by the city council without a vote of the citizens." He pointed to the evils growing out of legislative action by a few members of the city council and argued that the charter should be revised to give "citizens direct legislation in legislative matters."[50]

In addition to the mayor's efforts, businessmen and professionals organized a civic league and citizens' clubs in some wards. The avowed purpose of these clubs was to bring reform and thus graft-free government to Fort Worth. Reformers designed efforts to help offset the local political organization that controlled city politics. They held meetings throughout 1904 to drum up support for changes in the charter. The gatherings adopted resolutions opposing nepotism and favoring election of city department heads, initiative, referendum, maximum salaries for city officials, franchise tax, a separate school board, and tax exemptions to lure industry. One reformer declared that he had great faith in the ability of people, "who will think and act. They are the soul and body of any government. I don't believe that any one man or set of men know as much about the affairs of the city as the whole people." Fort Worth reformers believed that there should be only four or five aldermen, who "should be the very best businessmen to be found and elected by the people."[51] By stressing their faith in the ability of the people to judge, reformers hoped to convince the public that reform was a moral good and therefore a necessity for Fort Worth. The real intent was to gain control of city government from a council dominated by local and particularistic interests. If these alterations were adopted, reformers not only would control city government but also would make it more efficient and responsive to the needs of business.

The Board of Trade also sponsored meetings to arouse support for charter reform just before the opening of the legislature. These alleged "mass meetings" were in fact attended almost exclusively by leaders in business and the professions. The meetings endorsed the same reforms that Mayor Powell and the civic clubs had been advocating. Powell spoke to these sessions stressing the need for quick legislative action. He argued that the power of the city council should be diminished and vested instead in the hands of the people. At this time Powell and other reformers took an important step toward business control of Fort Worth city government. They began to advocate at-large elections for aldermen as the most effective means of limiting the power of professional politicians. They realized that only with city-wide elections could they defeat aldermen who owed allegiance to their respective wards.[52] At one gathering reformers even discussed commission government but dropped the subject in the belief that if the charter were amended to include their reforms they would win control of city affairs.[53]

Reformers organized a city-wide rally to win public endorsement for their new charter. At this meeting they added to their list of proposals election of all nine aldermen at large. Former Mayor Buckley B. Paddock argued that the city council should not be a legislative body, "but a business body." He thought that if aldermen were elected at large businessmen could be elected. Albert Baskins, a lawyer, agreed with Paddock, declaring that in city-wide election of aldermen there would be no "bartering or trading in the council." Reformers believed this plan would discourage both nepotism and the appointive power that permitted the building of "machines." The meeting passed a resolution asking the city council to adopt these changes in a new charter and forward it to the legislature.[54]

The city council considered these proposals and rejected most of them. In fact, the only change sought by the reformers that the council incorporated was a 2 percent tax on gross earnings from franchise holders. At one council meeting Powell pleaded for inclusion of the referendum on granting franchises. He contended that "if we could feel the pulse of the public of Fort

Worth" it would demand, as it had five years before, the initiative and referendum. He pointed out that every public meeting endorsed this reform. "I do not believe that any nine men . . . should have the right to give away franchises without a vote of the people." One alderman responded that the voters would not take the trouble to go and vote. He admitted the plan was popular but added, "how much responsibility has the average citizen in regard to municipal changes? He has no responsibility to bear and he is not to blame if the plan does not pan out successfully." Another considered it "our business to issue franchise, just as it is the business for people in a dry goods store to sell goods." Powell vetoed the council's charter but indicated that if the council included the referendum he would sign it. The council acquiesced, and the first of the reforms sought since 1900 was secured.[55]

This charter alteration represented only a minor victory for reformers. Again their attempt to persuade the city council by public pressure had failed. This setback convinced reformers that only through a complete revision of city government could they gain control of municipal affairs. It was out of this frustration that reformers decided to champion the virtues of commission government. Businessmen had tried to bring about change through the traditional form of city government but had failed. They now had to look for other alternatives.

Reformers organized additional civic clubs in wards previously without them. These clubs sought to obtain a new city charter and to elect businessmen to office.[56] At the same time Mayor Powell continued to speak out for charter revision. He declared that the referendum clause added to the present charter was a step in the right direction. Powell added that now the people had only themselves to blame if at anytime they did not have good government in Fort Worth. Time and again he pointed to the evils of the appointive system as opposed to civil service.

Powell saw no reason, for example, for sweeping changes in the police department after each election. The police should be free of "partisan politics." Under the present system the police department underwent rapid changes in personnel because the incoming marshall felt morally bound to reward his friends.[57]

Fort Worth reformers carried their campaign into the city primary election. Powell had announced his intention not to seek another term, thus placing an added burden on reformers, who had to find a suitable candidate who could lead them in the drive for charter revision. As the campaign opened, reformers made little mention of commission government. But they had every intention, once voters elected a new administration, to begin an all-out effort to bring it before the legislature in 1907. County Judge William Harris announced his candidacy for mayor on a platform of frugality in city affairs. He also disliked using the referendum for granting city franchises. He deplored the fact that the voters "felt they had to resort to it." The other candidate for mayor, Newton Lassiter, a successful lawyer and businessman, had the support of many leaders on the Board of Trade. He based his campaign on his intention to improve city services and conduct the office "by using businesslike methods in a businesslike way."[58]

The mayor's race did not represent a struggle between reformers and local politicians. In fact, both candidates had the support of reform groups. Little was said during the campaign about charter reform. The race boiled down to one between two personalities and in no way was it a referendum for reform. Instead, reformers, led by the businessmen of the Board of Trade, made an all-out effort to win control of the city council. They did not run candidates in all nine races but concentrated their efforts on a few key campaigns. Reformers told voters they needed more democracy, not less. These changes, they claimed, would give the people a greater voice in city affairs. By stressing their great faith in democracy, reformers hoped their opponents would be cast as antidemocratic. But Fort Worth voters did not respond to abstractions. Instead, they voted for men on the ward level who related to them and their problems. In only one race out of the four did reformers succeed in electing one of their own candidates. In all the other contests incumbents won renomination.[59] In the mayor's race Harris defeated Lassiter with 52.8 percent of the vote.[60]

Soon after the primary election, the Board of Trade began its campaign to bring commission government to Fort Worth. In its endorsement, the *Fort Worth Telegram* declared that voter ignorance of commission government was the greatest obstacle faced by the Board of Trade. To win over the "masses," the paper called for a campaign to educate the people thoroughly.[61] This was precisely the course the Board of Trade took. In a year-long effort reformers held meetings and published newspaper articles explaining the virtues of commission government. One reformer argued that salaries for city officials in Galveston, Texas, the first city to have commission government, were $28,280 compared to Fort Worth's $50,444. Clarence Ousley, editor of the *Fort Worth Record* and a former resident of Galveston, contended that commission government centralized city management, avoided delays in municipal affairs, prevented the advancement of one ward over another, and assured a "business administration." The new mayor, William Harris, also came out strongly in favor of the new system, as did outgoing Mayor Powell, who cited that the present government's chief fault "lies in the fact that it combines the legislative and executive functions."[62]

Civic clubs also joined in the campaign. The Sixth Ward Club declared at one meeting that the present government was inefficient and dominated by men who had only the interests of their wards in mind. Reformers cited the appointive power of the city council, which led to the development of "politics" in city affairs. Albert Baskins, one of the leaders in the reform movement, decided to run for the legislature so that he might bring a reform charter before that body when it met in 1907. With a reformer in Austin, the city council perhaps could be by-passed.

Baskins hoped to convince the legislature that commission government had the endorsement of all segments of Fort Worth society.[63] Former Mayor Thomas Powell thought the most effective means of creating this impression would be for the Board of Trade, civic league, bar association, city council, factory club, and Trade Assembly to appoint delegates to meet and draft a new charter. This document would then be submitted to the voters for their approval. Such a plan had several advantages, chief of which was that reformers would control such a "citizens committee." Mayor Harris quickly seized upon this idea. He called for these organizations to send delegates to his office to begin work on a charter. Albert Baskins, who had won in his legislative race in the July primary, came to the meeting with a draft of a commission-government charter.[64] Baskins had impressed the other legislators from Tarrant County with the need of his city for a new form of government. Throughout his campaign, he argued that commission government was the best form of "representative business government that can be framed for the management of municipal affairs." He contended that there was nothing in the commission idea that nullified local self-government. Five commissioners elected at large would be just as representative of Fort Worth as the nine aldermen elected in each of the wards. Commission government, he declared, "concentrates the authority and thus more definitely fixes responsibility of those charged with the management of affairs."[65]

Soon after the first meeting of the "citizens charter committee," a general outline began to emerge for commission government. The city council would consist of four commissioners and a mayor, who would serve as chairman of the board of commissioners, all of whom would be elected at large. The commissioners would have control and supervision over all city departments. The mayor would designate a commissioner over fire and police departments, streets and public property, and waterworks, sewage, finance, and revenue departments. The chief architect of this plan, Albert Baskins, declared that by handling city affairs in this fashion all departments would be brought directly and immediately under the supervision of the board of commissioners. "In this way," he said, "responsibility can be fixed absolutely on the commissioner in control of the department." In addition, the commissioners would have legislative powers. As their chief rationale for commission government, reformers in Fort Worth claimed that it concentrated and centralized the power of government in such a way as to give Fort Worth the most "effective, businesslike and economical government" possible.[66]

The final draft of the new charter provided strong powers for the board of commissioners to regulate utilities and to order the paving of streets.[67] Fort Worth businessmen had long wanted such powers for municipal government to allow the city to meet the demands for services from a rapidly growing industrial community. They believed that Fort Worth's ability to continue to attract people and industry rested upon the authority of city government to improve the community by paving the streets, increasing the water supply, and regulating municipal franchises. The new charter also provided for a separate school board elected at a different date than was the rest of city government.[68] This new charter would change the structure of Fort Worth city government so that the business community dominated and controlled it. Fort Worth business leaders wanted a government that could respond to their needs and provide efficient government at little cost to the taxpayers.

With the completion of the proposed new charter, the chief task of winning voter approval remained. Reformers decided that the legislature should pass the charter, then submit it to the voters. This would allow ample time to arouse public support and give voters a choice of voting for this proposed new charter or no new charter at all. By presenting commission government after its approval by the legislature, they apparently believed they could easily win voter approval.

Conversely, opponents tried to arrange a vote on the charter before it was sent to the legislature. The city council, as usual, led the opposition. The council, in fact, passed an ordinance providing for such an election. But Mayor Harris vetoed it, arguing that the cost would be too great and that the council lacked the authority to order such an election. The mayor pointed out that the real difference between the city council and the "citizens charter committee" was whether Fort Worth should have a commission form of government with enlarged powers or the city council with the same charter powers. The council easily overrode Harris's veto and set the election for January 23, 1907. A bitter struggle ensued that demonstrated the conflict between local politicians, who saw the ward system of election as the best method of representing the wishes of the people, and the business community, which wanted to gain political control of Fort Worth through at-large elections and a smaller city council.[69]

Reformers contended that under the present charter the council lacked the legal authority to call an election unless authorized by the legislature. Opponents admitted that this was true, but argued that the question was so important the election should be held anyway. Local politicians presented the city council with a petition from 807 voters who wanted a chance to vote on the charter before its passage by the legislature. But under pressure from the city's legal community, the council reversed its vote and declared in favor of allowing the people to vote on the charter after its approval in Austin.[70] The aldermen also decided to send the petition and their request concerning the timing of the election to the legislature in the hopes that body would believe the community badly divided and not vote on the proposed charter. Albert Baskins, however, refused to introduce the council's amendments.[71] The charter bill creating commission government sailed through the legislature without any opposition and the governor signed it into law February 26, 1907. The bill contained a provision that an election be held and the voters given at least twenty days' notice to vote on the new charter.[72]

Immediately after passage of the new charter, reformers began a campaign to rally support for it. Mayor Harris set the charter referendum for April 2, 1907. The Board of Trade and Civic League sponsored a series of "mass" meetings to arouse a popular brushfire for commission government. Former Mayors Paddock and Powell made several speeches throughout the city in favor of the new charter. Both men constructed their argument around the theme that the new government would centralize authority. They pointed out that department heads would be in control of their own affairs instead of having to await the meeting of the city council before acting. Mayor Harris supported an at-large election, declaring that all the people had a chance to vote for the entire board of commissioners. He held that the aldermanic system was not popular government, because a citizen could vote for only one alderman out of nine.[73]

Both the *Telegram* and the *Record* endorsed the new charter. The *Telegram* argued that the commissioners would work full time for the city and not have to "serve two masters." In addition, the various civic clubs in the city's wards made an all-out effort to canvass each registered voter and to provide him with a sample ballot.[74] They also organized committees to see that each voter got to the polls on election day. Reformers spared neither time nor money to see that their charter won approval April second.[75]

Opponents to commission government had little hope of defeating it. They lacked the organization and money needed to conduct a city-wide campaign that could compete with the proponents of commission government. Voters, who in the past had elected aldermen opposed to charter reform, lacked personal identification with any candidate. But, more important, voters could not see how the adoption of commission government affected their own self-interests. Opponents argued that at-large elections were undemocratic and not representative of the interest of each ward. They feared that concentrating power in the hands of four men would create a political oligarchy. Although some of these points later proved correct, voters in general viewed their arguments as abstractions.[76] Moreover, with the advent of the poll tax, many voters with low incomes, including most of Fort Worth's blacks, could not afford to pay the $1.00 yearly city poll tax. Out of a city population in 1907 of over 50,000 there were only 4,580 qualified voters. Another factor that worked in favor of the proposition was that only 56.4 percent of those qualified to vote took the trouble to do so. Therefore, the election results provided no surprise when commission government won overwhelmingly. In fact, 84.3 percent of those who voted favored the new charter, and it carried all nine wards by large majorities.[77]

Even before commission government had been approved, reformers had begun the second half of their program aimed at gaining control over municipal affairs. The Board of Trade organized the efforts of the business community to ensure that acceptable candidates were elected as commissioners. Business leaders decided that their best prospects lay in forming a "non-partisan slate," which implied that city elections should be above politics. By this method reformers associated partisan elections with the old aldermanic system, implying that such contests were immoral and corrupt. The idea that a nonpartisan slate was apolitical seems absurd when, in fact, reformers sought to win control of city hall by using campaign tactics that made reform a political issue. The Board of Trade issued a call for the various interests of Fort Worth, such as the civic clubs, factory club, lawyers, and Trade Assembly, to send delegates to a convention that would nominate candidates for mayor, board of commissioners, city attorney, and school board.[78] This so-called convention selected thirty delegates to form a ticket to be approved later by the entire body. Reformers asserted that the meeting "was non-partisan" and not one delegate was "one of the old time ward heelers." What everyone wanted to know, one reformer proclaimed, was whether "we are going to have a businessman's government for Fort Worth or a government by politicians."

Most of the candidates chosen by this "citizens committee" were prominent Fort Worth businessmen. The only exception on the commissioners' slate was Lee Stephens, a representative from the Trade Assembly. This sop to labor came as a result of their support over the years for the reforms advanced by the business community. The other members of the ticket included Mayor Harris, banker and manufacturer George Mulkey, real estate man and banker George Colven, and successful merchant and cattleman Sam Davidson. The nominees for city attorney and the school board came from the ranks of business and professions, with the only exception a union man as a candidate for the school board.

Fort Worth businessmen spared no effort to elect their ticket. The city's newspapers came out in support, civic clubs in the wards held meetings, ads were placed in newspapers, and employers pressured their men to vote the "correct" way. Moreover, labor unions held mass meetings to encourage workers to support the new charter.[79] After so many years of effort, reformers left nothing to chance in their effort to win political control of Fort Worth.

Little opposition to the business slate appeared. Many of the city's office holders who had been appointed by their aldermen faced the future with foreboding. They realized that under the new charter their prospects of job retention appeared dim. This was especially true of the police department, in which almost all the appointments had been political rewards. Some policemen and ward politicians tried to organize a slate of candidates to oppose the business, or "citizen," slate.[80] But they had little success. In a city-wide race they needed a large organization plus money and newspaper coverage. None of these was available. A ward politician could organize a campaign on the local level with little money by appealing personally to the particular interests of his ward. For this reason, opponents of the charter had little hope in a city-wide election, in which the local interests of the various wards were diluted.

The results of the election came as no surprise. The business slate swept "business government" into Fort Worth. In five races, mayor and commissioners, only two candidates opposed the "citizens ticket" and one of them was a disgruntled businessman. The other candidate, George Roberts, opposed George Mulkey, who had been mentioned as the probable police commissioner. In this race Mulkey soundly defeated Roberts, receiving 85.2 percent of the votes cast. The turnout of 55.8 percent for the election was excellent considering that little in the way of opposition was offered. The supporters of the reform slate had worked hard in canvassing the qualified voters and getting them to the polls. This effort paid off.[81]

With the victory of the "citizen ticket," Fort Worth businessmen could now go about moving the city in the direction they wanted. The business community was strongly committed to the principle of growth. They believed that, if Fort Worth could attract more industry and people, the city as a whole, as well as their own economic interests, would prosper. One step to achieve this end had been the establishment of business control over municipal affairs. The next step was to improve city services, such as sewer lines, paved streets, waterworks, police protection, sanitary regulations, and schools. Businessmen also set out to annex the suburbs surrounding Fort Worth. By incorporating such communities as North Fort Worth, Glenwood, Arlington Heights, and Rosen Heights, Fort Worth would increase vastly its population and create the image of a booming city that businessmen could use to bring more industry to Fort Worth.[82] Many of these goals were accomplished by 1910. But at what cost?

Fort Worth reformers, led by business and professional men, claimed that the changes they brought to municipal government would democratize city affairs. Had they not instituted the initiative, referendum, and commission government with at-large elections to give all voters equal opportunity to participate in city government? Yet, in spite of this ideology of democracy, Fort Worth reformers had set out as early as 1899 to alter significantly the political power structure of the city. The ward system of representation, which had given a political voice to the lower and middle classes through their own aldermen, had been destroyed. Now four commissioners elected at large sat where nine aldermen had once governed. The business community could now dictate who ran for office and, consequently, could exercise great influence in the decisions of city government. Only men with similar interests would be elected to sit on the city council. The business community thus had created a centralized city government attuned to its needs. But if it seemed more responsive to the business community, it was now less so to the needs of the lower class. No longer did the lower-class citizen feel he had anything in common with members of the city council; nor did he feel that they were looking out for his particular interests. He did not personally know any of the businessmen who served as commissioners and thus felt isolated from his local government. He had lost his identification with city government, for he could not relate his own experiences to the expanding city.

NOTES

1. George E. Mowry, *The Era of Theodore Roosevelt and the Birth of Modern America, 1900–1912*, pp. 59–85; Arthur S. Link, *Woodrow Wilson and the Progressive Era, 1910–1917*, pp. 1–25; Eric F. Goldman, *Rendezvous with Destiny: A History of Modern American Reform*, pp. 102–145; Richard Hofstadter, *The Age of Reform: From Bryan to F.D.R.*, pp. 174–215.

2. Harold A. Stone et al., *City Manager Government in the United States*; Frederick C. Mosher et al., *City Manager Government in Seven Cities*.

3. James Weinstein, "Organized Business and the City Commission and Manager Movements," *Journal of Southern History* 27 (May 1962): 166–182; Samuel P. Hays, "The Politics of Reform in Municipal Government in the Progressive Era," *Pacific Northwest Quarterly* 55 (October 1964): 157–169; James Weinstein, *The Corporate Ideal in the Liberal State, 1900–1918*, pp. 92–117. For a contrasting view, see Otis A. Pease, "Urban Reformers in the Progressive Era: A Reassessment," *Pacific Northwest Quarterly* 62 (April 1971): 53–55.

4. Weinstein, "Organized Business and the City Commission and Manager Movements," pp. 166–182; Hays, "Politics of Reform," pp. 157–169.

5. U.S. Bureau of the Census, *Twelfth Census of the United States: 1900. Population*, IV, 564–565; idem, *Thirteenth Census of the United States: 1910. Population*, IV, 232; see also Robert H. Talbert, *Cowtown Metropolis: Case Study of a City's Growth and Structure*, pp. 1–36. As a result of Fort Worth's heavy reliance on small manufacturing and trade, the city's labor force was chiefly semi- or unskilled.

6. Buckley B. Paddock, *History of Texas: Fort Worth and the Texas Northwest*; *History of Texas Together with a Biographical History of Tarrant and Parker Counties*; Sandra L. Myres, "Fort Worth, 1870–1900," *Southwestern Historical Quarterly* 72 (October 1968): 200–222.

7. *Twelfth Census of the United States: 1900. Population*, I, 476, 714, 798; *Thirteenth Census of the United States: 1910. Population*, Texas Supplement, p. 650.

8. Ibid.

9. U.S. Department of Commerce, *Census of Religious Bodies: 1906*, I, 440–442; idem, *Census of Religious Bodies: 1916*, I, 400–405.

10. Paddock, *History of Texas*, II, 623–626.

11. *Fort Worth Morning Register*, April 25, 1899.

12. Minutes of the Fort Worth City Council, Fort Worth City Hall, May 5, June 15, 1899; *Fort Worth Morning Register*, April 29, May 6, 9, June 16, 18, 1899.

13. James W. Spencer, president of the Farmer's & Mechanic's Bank, organized the Fort Worth Board of Trade during October 1899. Of its 132 original members, over 75 percent came from occupations that did business on a city-wide scale. They included officials from banking and real estate and owners of construction and merchandising concerns. The economic interest of these men was to see Fort Worth continue to grow and enlarge its scope of metropolitan activities. They did not limit themselves to narrow local concerns. Other members were drawn from the professions, such as doctors, educators, architects, and attorneys. See *Fort Worth Morning Register*, October 28, 1899; *Morrison and Fourmy City Directory of Greater Fort Worth, 1899–1909*; Paddock, *History of Texas*, passim.

14. *Fort Worth Morning Register*, July 9, 14, September 14, 1899; Paddock, *History of Texas*, II, 659–660.

15. See *Morrison and Fourmy City Directory of Greater Fort Worth, 1899–1909*; Paddock, *History of Texas*.

16. Alwyn Barr, *Reconstruction to Reform: Texas Politics, 1876–1906*, pp. 3–24; Julia K. Garrett, *Fort Worth: A Frontier Triumph*, pp. 235–305.

17. *Fort Worth Telegram*, August 27, 1905; "Fort Worth Federal Writers Project," IV, 1496–1500, Fort Worth Public Library.

18. *Fort Worth Morning Register*, December 3, 1899; "Fort Worth Federal Writers Project," VII, 2525–2527.

19. *Fort Worth Morning Register*, December 12, 1899.

20. Ibid., December 13, 1899.

21. Primary election results not available. See minutes of the City Council, April 16, 1900. In the general election held in April 1900, only 13.5 percent of the eligible voters went to the polls.

22. Minutes of the City Council, April 20, 1900.

23. *Fort Worth Morning Register*, September 6, October 13, 21, 1900; minutes of the City Council, May 4, 1900.

24. *Fort Worth Morning Register*, October 23, 1900.

25. Ibid., October 20; minutes of the City Council, April 20, 1900.

26. *Fort Worth Morning Register*, November 16, 1900; minutes of the City Council, November 16, 1900.

27. Minutes of the City Council, October 19, November 9, 13, 1900.

28. *Fort Worth Morning Register*, October 20, November 4, 10, 14, 16, 22, 23, 1900.

29. Minutes of the City Council, December 7, 1900; *Fort Worth Morning Register*, November 23, December 8, 1900.

30. Paddock, *History of Texas*, passim.

31. Minutes of the City Council, December 7, 1900; Frank Putman, "The Twin Cities of North Texas," *New England Magazine* 36, no. 6 (1907): 716–728.

32. *Fort Worth Morning Register*, December 11, 1900.

33. Ibid., February 14, 17, 19, 21, 24, 27, March 8, 23, 28, 29, April 14, 1901; minutes of the City Council, April 15, 1901.

34. Minutes of the City Council, April 19, 1901.

35. *Fort Worth Morning Register*, December 3, 4, 1901.

36. Ibid., December 9, 12, 19, 21, 1901.

37. Ibid., December 22, 1901.

38. Fort Worth does not fit the model used by Richard Wade and Zane Miller. According to Wade and Miller, reformers living in the outer ring of the city clashed with the ward bosses supported by immigrants and lower-class voters residing in the city's core. See Richard C. Wade, "Urbanization," in *The Comparative Approach to American History*, ed. C. Vann Woodward; Zane L. Miller, *Boss Cox's Cincinnati: Urban Politics in the Progressive Era*. Fort Worth's lower class was spread among most of the city's wards, and no ward had a high concentration of foreign born (*Twelfth Census of the United States: 1900. Population*, I, 476, 714, 798; *Thirteenth Census of the United States: 1910. Population*, Texas Supplement, p. 650).

39. *Fort Worth Morning Register*, April 19, 1902; *Fort Worth Telegram*, December 7, 1902, March 1, 4, 1903; minutes of the City Council, December 5, 1902, March 6, 1903.

40. *Fort Worth Morning Register*, October 5, 8, 1901; *Fort Worth Telegram*, March 16, 1903; Oliver Knight, *Fort Worth: Outpost on the Trinity*, pp. 173–175; Paddock, *History of Texas*, II, 659–660. North Fort Worth was incorporated November 18, 1902.

41. *Fort Worth Telegram*, December 7, 1902, March 1, 4, 8, 1903.

42. Barr, *Reconstruction to Reform*, p. 205; Donald S. Strong, "The Poll Tax: The Case of Texas," *American Political Science Review* 38 (August 1944): 693–709.

43. *Fort Worth Telegram*, January 22, February 1, 1903.

44. Ibid., January 13, 1904; *Fort Worth Morning Register*, December 22, 1901. The total vote cast in 1904 was only 58.8 percent of that in 1901. In fact only 50 percent of those registered voted.

45. *Fort Worth Telegram*, December 6, 8, 13, 37, 1903, January 7, 1904.

46. Ibid., January 13, 1904.

47. Ibid., March 2, 4, 18, 30, 1904.

48. Ibid., March 1, 3, 14, 29, 31, April 2, 4, 1904; *Fort Worth Record*, April 3, 1904.

49. Minutes of the City Council, April 11, 1904; *Fort Worth Record*, April 6, 1904.

50. Minutes of the City Council, May 6, 1904.

51. *Fort Worth Telegram*, May 29, November 26, December 21, 1904.

52. Ibid., October 3, 1903.

53. Ibid., December 1, 2, 5, 8, 21, 1904.

54. Ibid., December 28, 1904.

55. Minutes of the City Council, January 7, March 3, 13, 17, 1905; *Fort Worth Telegram*, March 4, 7, 11, 14, 1905.

56. *Fort Worth Telegram*, April 21, 25, 1905.

57. Minutes of the City Council, May 5, 1905; *Fort Worth Telegram*, July 10, 1905.

58. *Fort Worth Telegram*, November 14, 25, December 6, 1905.

59. Ibid., December 7, 9, 10, 11, 13, 15, 1905.

60. Ibid., December 15, 1905.

61. Ibid., March 3, 1906.

62. Ibid., March 2, 23, 28, 31, 1906; minutes of the City Council, April 10, 1906; H. J. Haskell, "The Texas Idea: 'City Government by a Board of Directors,' " *Outlook*, April 13, 1907, pp. 839–843.

63. *Fort Worth Telegram*, June 27, 30, 1906.

64. Ibid., September 11, October 4, 1906.

65. Ibid., September 14, 1906.

66. Ibid., October 5, 1906.

67. When the city council approved paving of a street, property owners along the street were assessed for the cost based on their frontage feet. The city paid only for intersections. The proposed charter would grant the council the power to make this assessment, an authority they lacked under the old charters.

68. *Fort Worth Telegram*, October 12, December 11, 14, 1906.

69. Minutes of the City Council, January 7, 12, 15, 1907; minutes of the Fort Worth Trade Assembly, January 16, 1907, University of Texas Library, Austin; *Fort Worth Telegram*, December 21, 1906, January 27, 30, 1907.

70. Minutes of the City Council, February 4, 1907.

71. Ibid., February 9, 18, 1907.

72. *Fort Worth Telegram*, February 13, 27, March 1, 1907; *Journal of the Texas House of Representatives*, Thirtieth Legislature, February 15, 1907, p. 492.

73. *Fort Worth Telegram*, February 28, March 3, 8, 16, 28, 1907; "Fort Worth Federal Writers Project," I, 167–168; *Fort Worth Record*, March 5, 1907.

74. *Fort Worth Record*, March 13, 14, 15, 16, 17, 18, 25, 28, 29, 1907.

75. *Fort Worth Telegram*, March 27, 28, 30, 31, 1907; *Fort Worth*

Record, March 3, 10, 1907; Samuel E. Kinch, Jr., "Amon Carter: Publisher-Salesman," M.J. thesis, University of Texas at Austin, 1965.

76. *Fort Worth Telegram,* February 28, March 10, 15, 1907.

77. Ibid., March 30, April 3, 1907; *Fort Worth Record,* April 3, 1907.

78. *Fort Worth Telegram,* March 4, 10, April 5, 6, 1907; *Fort Worth Record,* April 6, 1907; minutes of the Fort Worth Trade Assembly, April 5, 1907.

79. *Fort Worth Telegram,* April 10, 11, 13, 30, May 1, 1907; minutes of the Fort Worth Trade Assembly, April 5, 8, 11, 1907.

80. *Fort Worth Telegram,* April 14, 30, May 2, 3, 1907.

81. Minutes of the City Council, May 7, 1907; *Fort Worth Telegram,* May 3, 5, 1907.

82. See *Fort Worth Telegram, Fort Worth Record,* and minutes of the City Council 1908 and 1909 for the efforts by the Board of Trade to annex the suburbs.

BIBLIOGRAPHY

Barr, Alwyn. *Reconstruction to Reform: Texas Politics, 1876–1906*. Austin: University of Texas Press, 1971.

"Fort Worth Federal Writers Project." Fort Worth Public Library.

Fort Worth Morning Register, 1899–1902.

Fort Worth Record, 1904–1909.

Fort Worth Telegram, 1902–1909.

Garrett, Julia K. *Fort Worth: A Frontier Triumph*. Austin: Encino Press, 1972.

Goldman, Eric F. *Rendezvous with Destiny: A History of Modern American Reform*. New York: Alfred A. Knopf, 1956.

Haskell, H. J. "The Texas Idea: 'City Government by a Board of Directors.'" *Outlook*, April 13, 1907, pp. 839–843.

Hays, Samuel P. "The Politics of Reform in Municipal Government in the Progressive Era." *Pacific Northwest Quarterly* 55 (October 1964): 157–169.

History of Texas Together with a Biographical History of Tarrant and Parker Counties. Chicago: Lewis Publishing Co., 1895.

Hofstadter, Richard. *The Age of Reform: From Bryan to F.D.R.* New York: Alfred A. Knopf, 1955.

Journal of the Texas House of Representatives, 1907.

Kinch, Samuel E., Jr. "Amon Carter: Publisher-Salesman." M.J. thesis, University of Texas at Austin, 1965.

Knight, Oliver. *Fort Worth: Outpost on the Trinity*. Norman: University of Oklahoma Press, 1953.

Link, Arthur S. *Woodrow Wilson and the Progressive Era, 1910–1917*. New York: Harper & Row, 1954.

Miller, Zane L. *Boss Cox's Cincinnati: Urban Politics in the Progressive Era*. New York: Oxford University Press, 1968.

Minutes of the Fort Worth City Council, 1899–1909. Fort Worth City Hall.

Minutes of the Fort Worth Trade Assembly, 1907. University of Texas Library, Austin.

*Morrison and Fourmy City Directory of Greater Fort Worth, 1899–
    1909.*

Mosher, Frederick C., et al. *City Manager Government in Seven
    Cities.* Chicago: University of Chicago Press, 1940.

Mowry, George E. *The Era of Theodore Roosevelt and the Birth
    of Modern America, 1900–1912.* New York: Harper & Row,
    1958.

Myres, Sandra L. "Fort Worth, 1870–1900." *Southwestern Historical
    Quarterly* 72 (October 1968): 200–222.

Paddock, Buckley B. *History of Texas: Fort Worth and the Texas
    Northwest.* 4 vols. Chicago: Lewis Publishing Company, 1922.

Pease, Otis A. "Urban Reformers in the Progressive Era: A Re-
    assessment." *Pacific Northwest Quarterly* 62 (April 1971): 53–57.

Putman, Frank. "The Twin Cities of North Texas." *New England
    Magazine* 36, no. 6 (1907): 716–728.

Rice, Lawrence D. *The Negro in Texas, 1874–1900.* Baton Rouge:
    Louisiana State University Press, 1971.

Spratt, John S. *The Road to Spindletop: Economic Change in Texas,
    1875–1901.* Dallas: Southern Methodist University Press, 1955.

Stone, Harold A., et al. *City Manager Government in the United
    States.* Chicago: University of Chicago Press, 1940.

Strong, Donald S. "The Poll Tax: The Case of Texas." *American
    Political Science Review* 38 (August 1944): 693–709.

Talbert, Robert H. *Cowtown Metropolis: Case Study of a City's
    Growth and Structure.* Fort Worth: Leo Potishman Foundation,
    1956.

U.S. Bureau of the Census. *Twelfth Census of the United States:
    1900. Population,* vol. IV.

————. *Thirteenth Census of the United States: 1910. Population,*
    Texas Supplement.

U.S. Department of Commerce. *Census of Religious Bodies: 1906,*
    vol. I.

————. *Census of Religious Bodies: 1916,* vol. I.

Wade, Richard C. "Urbanization." In *The Comparative Approach
    to American History,* edited by C. Vann Woodward. New York:
    Basic Books, 1968.

Weinstein, James. "Organized Business and the City Commission and Manager Movements." *Journal of Southern History* 27 (May 1962): 166–182.

————. *The Corporate Ideal in the Liberal State, 1900–1918.* Boston: Beacon Press, 1968.

Historical Analogies and Public Policy: The Black and Immigrant Experience in Urban America

BY RICHARD C. WADE

HISTORICAL ANALOGIES are one of the games historians play. In its most serious exercise, it is the way scholars deepen insights into major historical problems. Stanley Elkins, for example, described certain aspects of the institution of slavery by equating them with Nazi concentration camps in World War II. Arthur Schlesinger illustrated the moral dimension of the coming of the Civil War by comparing the sectional conflict of the 1850's with the dilemma of democratic nations in the face of totalitarian aggression in the 1930's. Herbert Gans discovered an interesting parallel in Italian neighborhood life and its village antecedents in the old world. Not all analogies have been equally convincing, but at their best they provide an arresting perspective on persistent historical problems.

Analogies not only are a convenient construct of historians, but also provide a basis for making public policy. Leaders examine past experience while developing their own programs, using what they consider to be the "lessons of history" as a broad framework for contemporary action. Woodrow Wilson, for

instance, approached World War I from his historical understanding of the War of 1812. He had concluded from his own
work that President Madison had made a mistake in that conflict by bringing the United States into the war in effect on the
side of Napoleon and his imperial ambitions. Wilson always felt
that Madison had viewed the war too narrowly, seeing it as an
issue of freedom of the seas when he felt the deeper question
was the prospect of democracy and liberty in Europe. If the
young Republic could not avoid involvement, at least it ought
to have gone to war on the right side. When confronted with
another war a century later, Wilson faced the question of freedom of the seas for both sides. His reluctant neutrality always
tilted toward the Allies, and when Wilson did take the country
to war he raised it above the legal argument concerning international law and placed it on the high ideological ground of
the defense of democracy.

A better known analogy involves the famous Maginot line
in which the French believed that the lesson of its many wars
with Germany dictated a comprehensive defensive strategy. Ex-
pecting an analogous problem in the future, they created a
complex system of fortifications admirably designed to defend
France in 1870 or 1914, but which had become hopelessly dated
by 1939. And, of course, in diplomacy no word is more often
used than Munich. Referring to the Western betrayal of
Czechoslovakia during the European crisis in the thirties, it became a popular code word for the consequences of cowardice in
international affairs. This analogy was not simply invoked in
the same geographic area but was widely used by American
spokesmen in East Asia, Africa, and Latin America as well.

Historical analogies obviously are not always correct; indeed,
they can be misleading. But we do not know how to think about
big problems without them. They broaden our perspective, allow
us to put new problems into a more comfortable and intelli-

gible context, and remind us of the shared experience of others under similar circumstances either earlier or elsewhere. Sometimes these analogies are explicit, clearly stated by policy makers, and more or less precise in application. At other times, the analogy is assumed, perhaps being so apparent or so widely understood that it needs no elaboration.

I want to examine a case that falls into both these categories —a historical analogy that earlier lay unarticulated but assumed and later became the acting hypothesis of policy makers. Moreover, the problem involved is the most important facing the nation: the elemental question of race. The outlines of the issue need only restatement not elaboration.

Beginning at about the turn of the century, Southern blacks began to move into Northern cities. In one of the most massive migrations in history, Dixie's black population moved off the countryside into the nation's booming urban centers. For the past seventy-five years, the accommodation of these newcomers has been a central problem for city officials.

It was assumed by everyone that the blacks were simply the last of a whole series of migrants, and that what happened to the Irish, Germans, Italians, Poles, and Jews would also happen to Southern blacks. The same natural forces that had facilitated the acceptance of white newcomers would also ease the entrance of those from the South. And the public policies appropriate for the earlier groups would be applicable for the most recent arrivals regardless of race. The analogy was widely accepted and provided the framework for official thinking and action for the five decades when the blacks swarmed into Northern cities. The analogy, however, proved mistaken; the experiences of the white and black immigrants turned out to be fundamentally different.

The process by which the American city incorporated its European newcomers into municipal life is well known. The immigrants came from all over the old world. Most were poor and without marketable skills. As they piled into the crowded downtowns, they found housing where they could. Some owners carved small apartments out of old mansions, others converted rooms in warehouses, and still others constructed tenements for immigrant lodging. No space was too small for use. Whole families were stuffed into single rooms; unattached men made barracks out of basements. The population densities exceeded anything known before. New York's lower East Side had heavier concentrations than London, Paris, Naples, or even Bombay.

The crowding brought with it predictable consequences. Sanitation facilities, primitive at best, quickly became overburdened, and immigrant sections of town stood out on every health map drawn by city officials. Conditions coaxed disease; congestion permitted its rapid spread throughout the neighborhood. Quarantine required precisely the distance and space that were missing in the area. Hospital capacities were hopelessly small. No age or group was spared. In Chicago, one out of every three children in downtown precincts died by the age of one. Life, indeed, was mean, brutish, and short. By the nineties, public bodies and private agencies continuously published depressing accounts of slum conditions in every American city.

Moreover, jobs were scarce and unpredictable. Few newcomers could command much better than the least skilled work; most depended on seasonal employment. Ironically, the fact that so many people poured into cities forced municipal authorities into ambitious construction programs. New streets had to be paved, schools constructed, sewers put underground, bridges built, trolley lines laid, new city halls and court houses erected, and parks planned and developed. In short, the modern physical infrastructure of most American cities was built during the height of immigration. Since all this activity required unskilled labor on a grand scale, there were jobs enough to take the edge off want and desperation. Nonetheless, there were always too few jobs and too many mouths to feed.

The neighborhood had little to compensate for the congestion, inadequate housing, poor health, and low income of its residents. Schools were overcrowded, underfinanced, and usually poorly staffed. Religious organizations struggled vainly to provide enough buildings and schools for their growing numbers. Saloons alone kept pace with the population, dotting every street and forming a social focus for male activity outside the home. On the lower level, rampant crime and vice added danger and uncertainty to street life.

In short, conditions in immigrant ghettos in the late nineteenth and early twentieth centuries were never very pleasant. For the city, they were centers of continuous trouble, afflicted with wretched housing, erratic and low-paying jobs, inadequate schools, dirt and filth, high crime, and endemic disorder. Later these neighborhoods would be invested in retrospect with qualities their residents seldom knew. Writers and planners would find a benignancy in their clutter and crowding, in their intense ethnicity and religious diversity, and in their uncertain and fragile institutions. A whole nostalgic literature grew up in the sixties to contrast urban life of the present with what authors took to be true in 1900. But most of the "good old neighborhood" nostalgia would be written thirty years and sometimes thirty miles from childhood ghetto streets.

The fact is that most of the residents who could moved out into better areas in the city. Indeed, they found life tolerable in the old ghetto only because it was perceived to be temporary, a kind of staging ground for movement into an improved life elsewhere. And experience bore out this expectation. Every family knew of people who had once lived on the block and later found better quarters in another part of town. Sometimes it would be a member of the family, or perhaps someone in the parish, or a neighbor down the street, but the outward mobility was a continuing process. This fact was central to ghetto life because it made difficult conditions tolerable. If one could survive now, things might get better—at least for the younger ones. To be sure, the number "making it" comprised only a modest percentage, but the hope was more pervasive.

Constant movement, then, was a critical component of the immigrant ghetto. Scholars are just now discovering what residents knew so well; they are also beginning to gauge its extent. Howard Chudacoff's study of Omaha is, perhaps, the clearest account of this internal urban migration. Tracing immigrant mobility in the Nebraska boom town at the turn of the century, he concluded that "the overwhelming majority" of men living for twenty years in Omaha "occupied three or more homes" and only about 3 percent remained in the same dwelling for that period. Peter Knights and Stephen Thernstrom found the same movement among Boston's Irish in the nineteenth century, while Thomas Philpott's forthcoming volume on Chicago brilliantly demonstrates the universality of white immigrant residential instability in that polyglot metropolis.

Much of this residential movement was mere transience within the same neighborhood; some of it was forced by the tenant's inability to pay even small rents; and family additions required a constant search for larger quarters. Yet a significant amount represented genuine, if modest, social mobility. A better job and the accumulation of savings permitted purchase of a home in a better neighborhood farther away from the noise, congestion, and pollution of downtown. A single-family home or a two-flat replaced rooms in a crowded tenement or a converted mansion. Occasionally, the move was dramatic, involving a leap into a middle-class community well outside the original block. But usually the movement was gradual, involving several moves and many years. Nonetheless, the centrifugal action was unmistakable. Indeed, it was the genius of America's metropolitan system, allowing millions of people from different countries, with different languages and religions, to be incorporated into the nation's urban mainstream.

When blacks began to move into Northern cities on a large scale at the turn of the century, it was widely believed that they would repeat the process that had so successfully served millions of European immigrants. Policy makers assumed that the newcomers would, like their predecessors, concentrate in the center of cities, find some jobs, get an economic footing, discover their numbers, and slowly move outward toward the more pleasant residential areas of town. And, at first, it appeared that this calculation was correct. Blacks indeed did huddle in the congested center; jobs, while not plentiful or well paid, were available to some; and a group consciousness gradually emerged. Yet there was little outward movement; residential segregation increased with each decade and with each new wave of black migrants. Far from breaking, the ghetto held and expanded, oozing out into white neighborhoods on its borders. In the North this rigidity was new; in the South it was traditional.

In fact, the proper analogy for Northern cities was not the immigrant experience, but rather the black experience in Southern cities in the decades following the Civil War. For, in urban Dixie, blacks had been a substantial part of the population for at least four generations. In some cities the proportion reached almost half, seldom dropped below a quarter, and usually hovered around a third. Out of the tangled race relations bequeathed by the institution of slavery emerged a pattern that would later be re-created in Northern cities. An examination of that process will, I think, suggest something of the dimension of the race problem that so afflicts metropolitan America.

Even before slavery had been abolished, a system of segregation had grown up in Southern cities. The whites thought some

such arrangement was necessary if they were to sustain their traditional supremacy over the blacks in an urban setting. The
countryside provided enough room to give meaning to racial
separation. The master could be physically quite removed from
his blacks, though sharing the same plantation or farm. And together both were isolated from others. In cities these spatial re-
lationships were quite different. Both races were thrown together; they encountered each other at every corner; they rubbed
elbows at every turn; they divided up, however inequitably, the
limited space of the town site. Segregation sorted people out by
race, established a public etiquette for their conduct, and created social distance where there was physical proximity. Urban
circumstances produced this system long before the destruction
of slavery itself.

Of course, the complete separation of races was impossible in
the city, and practices differed from place to place. In some
towns, public conveyances remained mixed; in others Negroes
were not excluded from all public grounds; in still others housing continued scrambled. Yet every city developed its own arrangement expressed in the contrived separation of black and
white in countless ways. Though never total, the segregation was
so extensive that blacks were never permitted to forget their
inferior position.

The rising incidence of segregation characterized race relations even before emancipation. Rooted in the white's need for
discipline and deference, it developed to take up the slack in the
loosening system of slavery. It provided public control to replace
the dwindling private supervision of master over slave. To do
this, the difference between free and enslaved blacks had to be
narrowed, depriving the free of part of their freedom even while
permitting a wider latitude to bondsmen. To most whites, however, there seemed no alternative. The old system no longer

really controlled; the walls no longer really confined; the chains no longer really held.

After the Civil War, the South had to produce a new system of race relations. Slavery was dead, and, except for the nascent segregation in the cities, there were no guidelines to inform public policy. In the countryside the problem was not as acute; space provided racial separation. Local governments had very limited jurisdiction—schools, roads, almshouses—which required no immediate racial decisions. The schools would, of course, be segregated but the broader question of a new racial system was not so urgent. But in the cities the question could not be postponed. Blacks in large numbers, landless and unskilled, drifted from the countryside into the cities. Local authorities were overwhelmed by this migration. They had neither the facilities nor a program to deal with the new situation. Yet they had to act, and in the racial assumptions underlying their response lay the seeds of modern urban segregation.

A close look at the development of race relations in Atlanta perhaps best illustrates the case. As the capital of Georgia, it lay in the heart of Dixie; as a city leveled by the war, it had to start from scratch in both its physical and its social rebuilding. To be sure, as a small town in the fifties, it had been governed by the institution of slavery, and its race relations looked very much like those in other Southern cities. Yet emancipation and destruction offered a new opportunity to find a racial system appropriate for a new South.

By 1870 Atlanta's population was about 40 percent black, a proportion that has remained stable until our own times. The crisis in the young city was immediate. Former slaves came into the city as soon as the war ended. Most had no skills, and jobs were scarce. As a result the number of poor mounted rapidly, forcing the city to produce facilities for their care. From the beginning, local authorities established separate almshouses, initially by leasing and then with new construction. Vagrancy was inevitably the handmaid of poverty, and blacks picked up for loitering were placed in custody. They were then taken before a separate court, and, if guilty, placed in segregated quarters in the jail. Later a black facility replaced the single institution.

Inevitably, of course, many blacks became sick. The city needed hospital care for both races but lacked the money to construct two buildings. Hence, they erected only one; yet, the new facilities included separate rooms and separate entrances. Whites entered from the main street and blacks by the side door. Inside, segregated quarters served whites and blacks in different parts of the hospital. Inevitably, too, the newcomers would die, and, just as separate as in life, blacks would be interred in separate plots. In the years before the war the city's central cemetery had a quadrant reserved for the black dead. But in 1871 a new area was set aside on the west end, and, in the cool notation of the city council minutes, the bones of blacks were dug up and moved to the new area. Moreover, for the nameless or poor, separate pauper fields were available.

In short, when public policy had to be made to meet clear exigencies, the racial assumptions of local officials were abundantly clear. They believed in the separation of the races and they devised elaborate means to keep black and white apart. Moreover, all this happened in the Reconstruction South under federal supervision when official statements gave presumption to equality. Yet, when confronted with very practical problems and the need to act, white officialdom opted for segregation.

Educational development revealed the same tendencies. From the outset white and black students attended different schools. Black teachers taught only in their own system, though whites occupied both the school board and, until the 1890's, all the principals' chairs. Moreover, public library facilities excluded blacks from the beginning. In Atlanta this handicap was not as fatal as elsewhere, because what would later become Atlanta University offered a whole range of education not available to blacks elsewhere in the South. Yet any learning in the Georgia capital took place in segregated units.

The development of parks displayed the same racial policy. Small parks created no problem since they were easily segregated, but larger ones needed interior separation to separate the races. When a zoo was established, authorities met the delicate problem by keeping visitors separated by the central cages where, as the *Atlanta Constitution* observed with satisfaction, "an aisle 7 feet wide was railed off on each side of the cages— one for whites, and the other for blacks," and "there is no communication between them." Thus the occupation of open space as well as the more congested places demonstrated the same racial assumption.

Quasi-public facilities also fell into separate categories. In the theaters, blacks entered by different doors, occupied designated areas, and fended for themselves for refreshments. Hotels and restaurants excluded them, and except for a few downtown bars the color line also prevailed. Occasionally a traveler, especially if politically connected, would be accommodated for a short time, but in 1872 the Calhoun opened to meet "a necessity long felt by colored citizens" because the "better class" of blacks would not travel due to the "ill and unjust treatment" they suffered at the hands of "public carriers and innkeepers . . . who claim the right to discriminate." When the horse-drawn street car was introduced in the same year, it adopted the same restrictions.

Employment and housing involved less overt public policy. Moreover, the legacy of slavery in these areas was more ambivalent. Yet the trend in both was the same—toward more separation. Under the peculiar institution, workers mingled on many jobs and, though blacks usually did the most menial tasks, 6 percent were classified as skilled in 1870. Georgia law had reserved most of the high-paying skills for whites in antebellum years, but the postwar practice began with some mixing. As the decades wore on, however, exclusion became more frequent and even the small percentage of black skilled labor almost disappeared.

Residential segregation was similarly a result of white practice with some public encouragement. Before abolition, blacks and whites had shared the same urban plot, and though the slaves lived in back quarters, racial proximity was a central fact. Over the three decades after emancipation another residential pattern emerged. A racial map of 1870 showed blacks living in all parts of Atlanta. To be sure, there were heavier concentrations on the east and south sides. But only a few blocks were wholly black. By 1880 the new system became visible. Black residents in the northern part of the city diminished, and the areas of full black occupancy expanded. It was then possible to identify the "colored sections" of town. After ten more years the present areas of concentration appeared clearly. Eastern downtown areas —"buttermilk bottom" and "sweet Auburn"—were wholly black. The area around Atlanta University on the west side had developed as a homogeneous community. Elsewhere in the city, some residual black residents could be found scattered throughout white neighborhoods. Yet the tendency was clear: the index of racial segregation in housing rose with each census. By 1890 the shape of the modern ghettos had been fixed.

Just as revealing was the racial composition of new housing. Atlanta was one of the great boom towns of the new South with a population that jumped from 9,500 in 1860 to 37,500 in 1880 to 65,000 in 1890. This expansion required new residential building, most of which took place on the outer edges of town where land was vacant and cheap. In these new areas all the construction was for whites. Areas later annexed by the city had no black residents at all. The meaning was clear enough: when whites had a choice they moved into racially exclusive areas. Blacks were more and more confined to the old areas of town with hand-me-down buildings or jerry-built wooden dwellings. The historic urban forces that have produced the white ring around the black center had begun; the modern ghetto appeared even before the present century.

By 1885 race relations in Atlanta had been set. Over two decades a series of public decisions and private practices created a pervasive pattern of segregation. Though there were a few crevices, the system left little room for leakage. At any moment blacks were confronted with discrimination. Whether it was in a public facility, school, or church, or on the job, their "place" was clear. Moreover, whites believed that blacks liked it that way. Revealing both local customs and the official view, the *Atlanta Constitution* asserted: "We believe that negroes themselves do not, and would not if they had the power, insist on miscellaneous assemblages. Here in Atlanta they have their own churches, are ministered by their own pastors and conduct their own affairs. . . . In this city they have their own schools, equal in all respects to white schools. . . . They have their own secret societies of Odd Fellows, Masons, military companies and societies. . . . They have their own restaurants, hotels and largely their own doctors, lawyers and merchants. This is the proper adjustment of this matter in our opinion."

What happened in Atlanta developed in other Southern cities, though, of course, with variation. Not all places segregated the same categories. Some permitted mixing in a few public places or on street cars; others never separated the races in theaters or parks; and in the more stagnant postwar towns, such as Charleston, it took longer to untangle housing and employment patterns. Yet by 1880 the urban South was effectively segregated. No matter where the black might turn, on the street, in the school or church, in recreational or health facilities, on his job or in his neighborhood, he was reminded of the general white judgment that the races ought to be separate. This public etiquette governed behavior everywhere and was embodied in numberless ordinances and governmental regulations. Later Jim Crow laws formalized this segregation on a statewide level.

This development was fixed by the time the great black migration began to Northern cities. And it would be repeated there. When the vanguard got to Chicago, for example, it found blacks living in many parts of the city. To be sure, most lived in minighettos in out-of-the-way locations and suffered racial discrimination in many ways. But the numbers were small and whites felt no general threat. As the migration mounted, however, so did the separation. The newcomers flocked into the south and west sides. Low incomes and real estate practices confined black residents to certain areas. In 1917, the real estate board formally embodied the segregation by declaring it a violation of its rules to sell to blacks outside the concentrated areas. School board policy, using district line changes and branch schools, separated youngsters in public education. Whites living near black neighborhoods resisted the spread of the ghetto, often with violence. In 1919 a race riot revealed the grim dimensions of Chicago's ghetto as it fractured the town's racial peace.

A similar pattern developed in other Northern cities. As the proportion of blacks rose so did the size of the ghetto. Unlike in the South, public policy seldom consciously underwrote the process; indeed, even as the separation proceeded, public officials condemned segregation and city councils legislated against discrimination. No one denied the problem; in fact, government reports laid it out in agonizing details and sponsored programs to foster equality. Political rhetoric warned against creating

Southern relations in Northern metropolises. Yet, inevitably, the ghetto grew, absorbing white neighborhoods as it spread. Through the century, the index of residential segregation rose and the distinction between North and South narrowed. By 1950 every city of considerable size had its black sector.

This new black ghetto was fundamentally different from the old immigrant ghetto. Unlike its earlier white counterpart, the new ghetto did not disperse part of its population into other parts of the city. The escape valve of the immigrant concentrations was missing; the black areas simply filled up and spread out. The earlier ghetto had been tolerable because its residents thought it temporary; the new ghetto became intolerable because its inhabitants increasingly considered it permanent. Initially, blacks thought escape was always possible and that hard work, education, and some luck would spring at least their most successful into the middle-class white world beyond. The last generation has seen this hope fade and the ghetto triumph.

This confinement produced two consequences that were new. The first was the increasing embitterment of the rising black middle class, which became increasingly frustrated by the intractability of residential restrictions. After all, they had met every traditional criteria for acceptance. They had education, good employment, and considerable income. Yet they were denied the most important symbol of American success—the right to live where they wanted, in neighborhoods of their own choosing with schools appropriate to their children's abilities or their own ambitions. They now learned that the only basis of their exclusion was the color of their skin. A college degree and a substantial income could carry the black family into better housing but, with a few exceptions, not into genuinely integrated communities. When the white middle class abandoned the city, the suburbs offered competitive possibilities. For the emergent blacks that option only occasionally appeared.

Ironically, the excluded comprised one of the most successful classes in American history. No other group had produced such a large middle class in such a short period of time as did the North's urban blacks. In 1950 the federal census classified their proportion as about 8 percent; by 1960 that figure more than doubled; in 1970 the black middle class in the cities comprised one-third of their total. In places like Chicago and Los Angeles the percentage exceeded forty. There are, of course, problems with the census definition, especially because black middle-class families frequently involved two breadwinners. But this fact simply underlined the ambition of the new group at the same time it added some ambiguity to the figures.

The civil rights revolution of the fifties and early sixties was led by this energetic, intelligent, and embittered middle class. After more conventional strategies failed, this group, despairing of breaking the ghetto, turned inward to organize it. This had not happened with immigrant graduates of the ghetto, who quickly identified themselves with their new communities and gradually loosened their ties with the old neighborhoods. As the Irish, for example, fled the ghetto they might send some money back to the church, keep a few memberships in old associations, and drop in on St. Patrick's Day. But the focus of family life was in the new area and what lay ahead there for the family. The black middle class was never offered that opportunity. Denied a new community, they turned back into the old.

Here they discovered the second major difference between the new and old ghettos. The young, often now a majority in black neighborhoods, had already given up on the system. A young boy of fourteen could look around and say to himself: "What difference does it make for me to do what they tell me to. All around are people who did that. They stayed in school and out of trouble; they got their jobs and money. But they are still just like we are—living in bad neighborhoods with vice, crime, and rip-offs, bad schools, high prices, and impossible rent. What difference does it make what *I* do?" Nearly every poverty program in the sixties floundered on the question of motivation. "Why don't they act like the Italians, Irish, Poles, and Jews did?" is the familiar bureaucratic lament. But the answer is clear: they were never treated like Italians, Irish, Poles, and Jews. In this fact lie the hopelessness, frustration, and feckless violence of the American city.

The ghettos erupted in the sixties when the frustrated young people struck out at what appeared to them to be the oppressor. Though most of the deaths, injuries, and damages were suffered by blacks in black neighborhoods, the mutiny shook white America and damaged, at least temporarily, the fragile racial bonds of the country. What was significant through those grim years was the retrospective sampling of black middle-class opinion. In large numbers, they deplored violence, noting that the casualties were almost always black. At the same time, however, they refused publicly to denounce the rioters, because they said they understood the causes that lay behind the explosion. The Italian American middle class, on the other hand, has always been anxious to separate themselves from illegal action, especially the Mafia, when it tends to reflect adversely on the whole group within the wider community. The new ghetto has denied its successful middle class the luxury of those internal distinctions.

Moreover, the shape of the black ghetto frustrated political attempts to lessen tensions and provide an orderly dissolution of the infected spots. For the black neighborhoods almost invariably abutted on low-income white residential areas. The people living there had already moved several times before and now lacked the resources for the final leap into the suburbs. Resistance was everywhere strong; in places it was marked by violence. The racial guerilla warfare in these urban communities shattered the Democratic party and encouraged a new demagoguery. The disintegration of central policy making resulted in endless vetoes applied by one local group or another on city, state, and national programs.

In the larger context, the situation was almost bizarre. Race was, and is, the country's most persistent and dangerous problem. Yet it was being determined by the group least able to handle it. The white residents at the edge of the ghetto are among the least educated, have the lowest incomes, and are the most insecure people in American society. Yet the nation places on their backs its most difficult question. Meanwhile, those with the highest education, greatest resources, and most security are far removed from the battle. And from the safety of the suburbs they judge the merits of the contesting forces, chiding the blacks with being too militant and labeling blue-collar whites as "backlashers." Hence, the decision on race, surely the most delicate and explosive of this century, reposes in the hands of people whose margins of maneuver are very thin.

The new ghetto thus upsets expectation. Its intractability is new and obviously dangerous. What is now important is to devise a new national housing program that takes into account the difference between the black and immigrant experiences in American cities. The most recent newcomers will need a new policy designed to break the walls of the ghetto and permit their residents to disperse throughout the metropolis. The beginning of wisdom in developing a new approach is to drop the immigrant analogy and to understand that, if the old historical forces continue to govern residential patterns, the indices of segregation will continue to rise and the ghetto will continue to fester.

The present condition contrasts sharply with the historic situation. The public policy so successful in incorporating immigrant millions into metropolitan America has proved inappropriate for the blacks. Indeed, continuing the old responses merely aggravates the new tensions. The Federal Housing Authority, for example, has developed practices that encourage new home building away from the central city while minimizing commitments to downtown residential rehabilitation. This policy, always somewhat controversial, has become disastrous because it further depresses ghetto areas and facilitates the white flight from the city. The earlier dependence on used housing for low-income people no longer works, because race considerations interfere with the free exchange of dwellings in the hand-me-down market. Slum clearance and urban renewal programs merely tighten the black housing market without sufficient replacements of new units.

Nor will it be enough merely to "improve" the ghettos. The "model cities" programs were an elaborate and expensive attempt to make life in the inner neighborhoods tolerable if not comfortable. The slogan, "community control," added to the attractiveness of this strategy because it seemed more democratic and professed to offer power to the hitherto powerless. But ghetto communities simply do not have the resources to become self-sufficient and to "run their own affairs." They are by definition areas without enough jobs, with inadequate schools and hospitals, and with noncompetitive shopping. The tax base is too small to provide the most elementary services, much less to revive a rundown part of town. The only feasible road to genuine equality lies in opening up the outer areas to black residents. Not only does justice demand it, but also, as a practical matter, the blacks will not settle much longer simply for a slice of the slum.

The easiest remedy will also be the most effective. A new national housing policy should simply stipulate that any public subsidy for multiunit dwellings provide for 10 to 15 percent low- and moderate-income families. This proposal would cover any subsidy whether it be overt—such as FHA loans, tax write-offs, or below-market mortgages—or covert, such as the building of streets, sewers, water mains, or lighting. Present practice now subsidizes all kinds of people who need no help: the developers, the banks, and high-rent tenants. In fact, since the average unit of housing now exceeds $30,000, we will have to subsidize in some manner even middle-income families just to maintain our present stock. This new policy should say to the developer: "If you want a public subsidy, you also take public policy; if not, you are free to build on your own and charge the full market price to your owner or tenant. Find your own mortgage money, pay full taxes, and build your own facilities." Moreover, this requirement would apply to suburban development as well as city construction.

The result would be a gradual dispersion of low-income families of both races throughout the metropolitan area. It would spread the burden everywhere instead of aggravating the old neighborhoods at the edge of the ghetto, or singling out a few suburbs here and there to make adjustments. Indeed, if we had operated under such a policy since 1960, the present dangerous concentrations would have already been reduced and a significant part of the black middle class would have found housing in pleasant residential areas. While segregation would no doubt remain beyond acceptable levels for some time, at least the edge of racial bitterness would be blunted and the permanence of the ghetto challenged.

Moreover, such a housing policy is also an antipoverty strategy, for it provides local remedies for poor families. Part of the intractability of ghetto problems is the concentration of all urban ills in one area—bad shelter, inadequate schools, unsafe health facilities, high prices, rampant vice and crime. A great social bonus of fair housing would accrue by placing low-income families in decent neighborhoods where they would benefit from institutional support, now so difficult to create in the ghetto. They would live where the schools are better, clinics and hospitals are within walking distance, household prices are somewhat regulated by competitive shopping, and police and fire protection are more efficient. Much of the public money now thrown into depressed areas could then be used to subsidize new housing in better neighborhoods instead of supporting compensatory programs in the ghetto. Moreover, in spreading the burden of the problem throughout the metropolis, we would also heighten the responsibility of those now geographically removed from the consequences of present policy and practice.

This new urban policy would, of course, require sacrifices, but at least they would be borne by everyone. And let us be clear on the alternative. If we continue to draw a white noose around black downtown, we invite racial confrontation and violence. The relative tranquility of the past few years stems not from a new level of justice but rather from a temporary resignation. The same conditions that caused the explosions of the sixties are still embedded in ghetto life like a time bomb ticking away. We ought not be complacent now, but rather use these precious years in creating new policies that will begin the dissolution of our urban ghettos. In so doing, we would not only be prudent, but we also could help to redeem that pledge of human equality so eloquently expressed in Philadelphia almost two centuries ago.